DAYS OF
RECKONING

DAYS OF
RECKONING

Young Canadians discover how decisions by the older generation have jeopardized the country's future

EDITED BY
JOHN WOOD

BREAKOUT EDUCATIONAL NETWORK
IN ASSOCIATION WITH
DUNDURN PRESS
TORONTO · OXFORD

Copyright © Breakout Educational Network, 2003

www.breakout-ed.net

Publisher: Inta D. Erwin
Copy-editor: Amanda Stewart, First Folio Resource Group
Designer: Bruna Brunelli, Brunelli Designs
Printer: Webcom

National Library of Canada Cataloguing in Publication Data

Days of reckoning/edited by John Wood.

One of the 16 vols. and 14 hours of video which make up the
underground royal commission report
Includes bibliographical references and index.
ISBN 1-55002-418-3

1. Debts, Public—Canada—Public opinion. 2. Budget deficits—
Canada—Public opinion. 3. Fiscal policy—Canada—Public opinion.
4. Debts, Public—Canada. 5. Budget deficits—Canada. 6. Fiscal
policy—Canada. I. Wood, John. II. Title: underground royal
commission report.

JL65.D398 2002   336.3'4'0971   C2002-902298-3

1   2   3   4   5   07   06   05   04   03

Printed and bound in Canada.
Printed on recycled paper. ♻
www.dundurn.com

This book is the companion volume to the video series *Days of Reckoning*, produced by Stornoway Productions Inc.

Exclusive Canadian broadcast rights for the *underground royal commission* report

intelligent television

Check your cable or satellite listings for telecast times

Visit the *urc* Web site link at:
www.ichanneltv.com

About the *underground royal commission* Report

Since September 11, 2001, there has been an uneasy dialogue among Canadians as we ponder our position in the world, especially vis à vis the United States. Critically and painfully, we are re-examining ourselves and our government. We are even questioning our nation's ability to retain its sovereignty.

The questions we are asking ourselves are not new. Over the last 30 years, and especially in the dreadful period of the early 1990s, leading up to the Quebec referendum of 1995, inquiries and Royal commissions, one after another, studied the state of the country. What *is* new is that eight years ago, a group of citizens looked at this parade of inquiries and commissions and said, "These don't deal with the real issues." They wondered how it was possible for a nation that was so promising and prosperous in the early 60s to end up so confused, divided, and troubled. And they decided that what was needed was a different kind of investigation — driven from the grassroots 'bottom,' and not from the top. Almost as a provocation, this group of people, most of whom were affiliated with the award winning documentary-maker, Stornoway Productions, decided to do it themselves — and so was born the *underground royal commission*!

What began as a television documentary soon evolved into much more. Seven young, novice researchers, hired right out of university, along with a television crew and producer, conducted interviews with people in government, business, the military and in all walks of life, across the country. What they discovered went beyond anything they had expected. The more they learned, the larger the implications grew. The project continued to evolve and has expanded to include a total of 23 researchers over the last several years. The results are the 14 hours of video and 16 books that make up the first interim report of the *underground royal commission*.

So what *are* the issues? The report of the *underground royal commission* clearly shows us that regardless of region, level of government, or political party, we are operating under a wasteful system ubiquitously lacking in accountability. An ever-weakening connection between the electors and the elected means that we are slowly and irrevocably losing our right to know our government. The researchers' experiences demonstrate that it is almost impossible for a member of the public, or in most cases, even for a member of Parliament, to actually trace how our tax dollars are spent. Most disturbing is the fact that our young people have been stuck with a crippling IOU that has effectively hamstrung their future. No wonder, then, that Canada is not poised for reaching its potential in the 21st century.

The *underground royal commission* report, prepared in large part by and for the youth of Canada, provides the hard evidence of the problems you and I may long have suspected. Some of that evidence makes it clear that, as ordinary Canadians, we are every bit as culpable as our politicians — for our failure to demand accountability, for our easy acceptance of government subsidies and services established without proper funding in place, and for the disservice we have done to our young people through the debt we have so blithely passed on to them. But the real purpose of the *underground royal commission* is to ensure that we better understand how government processes work and what role we play in them. Public policy issues must be understandable and accessible to the public if they are ever to be truly addressed and resolved. The *underground royal commission* intends to continue pointing the way for bringing about constructive change in Canada.

— Stornoway Productions

14 hours of videos also available with the *underground royal commission* report. Visit Stornoway Productions at www.stornoway.com for a list of titles.

TABLE OF CONTENTS

FOREWORD

In late August of 1994 Kit Vincent, an old friend from university days, rang and invited me to lunch. He was, among other things, the executive producer of his own film company, Stornoway Productions, in Toronto.

During the 1980s Stornoway, named after the town in the Scottish Hebrides, not the Ottawa home of the leader of the Opposition, had developed some original and ambitious documentary projects, many of them about the effects of the cold war around the world. My career had been largely in the theatre but I was also interested in documentary films. During the previous three years I had attended occasional brainstorming sessions at Stornoway with a number of other people, including Richard Nielsen, at which we tried to help Kit develop an idea for an investigative documentary project targeting the emerging problems confronting Canada. Kit had seen these problems coming for a lot longer than we had, and he was determined to use his resources to identify them, examine their origins and, most importantly, find a way to solve them. He jokingly called this project the *underground royal commission*.

I missed a number of these meetings when I was away directing, and quite often lost touch with the project's developments.

In 1994 I was tackling a musical at the Elgin Theatre in Toronto called *Napoleon*. Although it had only a short life and took years from mine, trying to figure out how to get the "little general" and his army across the Alps on the stage of the Elgin was nothing compared to what was thrown to me by Kit on that late summer day three months after the musical had folded.

He had decided on a course of action.

He was ready to take the first bold step, which would be a cross-country film venture examining, among other things, the policies of various Canadian governments over the past 30 years. It would be an effort to determine what their actions, especially their fiscal programs, meant to the future of young people just emerging from university and, of course, to the future of the country. The film would feature some recent graduates as researchers and on-camera interviewers, but Kit was adamant that they should not be professional or experienced journalists. "Who are they?" I asked. He didn't know. Part of my job would be to find them. "When do we start shooting?" He smiled. "At the end of September. You've got a month to get ready!"

I quickly began to put together a production team with the help of friends who had more experience in television than I and who knew the Toronto scene better. The major task I faced was finding the young interviewers. Putting together a group that could be prepared and start to travel in less than a month was daunting, to say the least. I interviewed nearly 50 people over the next couple of weeks in Toronto and Ottawa. We narrowed our list down and the seven we chose all represented different parts of the country and came to the project with a grand variety of loud political opinions. After a brief and highly charged period of preparation, we hit the road and headed for the centre of the country, Manitoba.

Over the next six months we covered the country, stopping in every province and talking to a cross-section of people from all walks of life. Although the members of the team started the trip as green and inexperienced journeymen, they quickly grew into knowledgeable and determined researchers and interviewers. However, they never lost the openness and honest enthusiasm with which they began and which prompted so many people to be utterly candid and forthright with them.

It is now eight years since we made our journey. I had travelled across Canada many times before, but this trip resulted in a view of the land which will never be replaced. It was as beautiful as ever and the people we met were optimistic and friendly, but what I heard from many of them often depressed and discouraged me. The rose-coloured glasses came off when I realized that, as with most Canadians, I had gone through the last 25 years without knowing what was really happening in and to my country.

Since 1994, this project has moved far beyond what I had initially envisioned. *Days of Reckoning* was the beginning of a journey that has led to subsequent adventures and discoveries. But it was the starting point and anything we've learned since we were able to understand because we spent six months listening to people who knew a hell of a lot more than we did.

This book is a collection of some of the comments on a wide range of subjects heard by the team as they gathered the material for the television documentary. In the best sense it is a history book, although that description may relegate it, at least in the minds of some, to dusty and hidden corner shelves. But the stories which emerged from this journey are as timely today as they were when we recorded them. While some of the industries or situations we investigated have changed somewhat over the past few years (for example, The Workers' Compensation Board of Ontario, SYSCO in Cape Breton and Ontario Hydro), the lessons we learned are revealing and still very relevant.

The researchers' presence in this book is not nearly as prominent as it was in the film documentary, but their questions and introductions honestly reflect the cheeky humour with which they greeted each new challenge. While the book is by them and those people who agreed to speak so openly, it's really about Canadians — all of us.

John Wood
Stratford, Ontario
June 2002

—— People Who Spoke to Us ——

Charles Adams, a tax historian, author and beekeeper, is an adjunct scholar with the Ludwig von Mises Institute — an economic think tank — at Auburn University in Alabama. He is the author of *For Good and Evil*, which examines the relationship between governments, people and taxes. His new book, *When in the Course of Human Events*, for which he won the 2000 Paradigm Book Award, is about the role of the South in the American Civil War.

Ted Allen is president of Agricore United, formerly United Grain Growers, in Winnipeg.

Miller Ayre is the publisher of *The St. John's Telegram*.

Ian Baines is president and chief operations officer of Canadian Renewable Energy Corporation.

Louis Balthazar has been a professor in political science at Laval University in Quebec City since 1969. He was the co-editor of the Department of External Affairs publication *International Perspectives* from 1974 to 1981. He has published extensively on U.S.–Canada relations and Quebec nationalism.

Colin Beasley is the former president and chief executive officer of International Wallcoverings in Brampton, Ontario. He is now retired.

JOE BEWS is a third-generation farmer and rancher in Longview, Alberta.

PAUL BROWN is a professor of public administration at Dalhousie University in Halifax.

ELIZABETH BRUBAKER is the executive director of Environment Probe, a division of Energy Probe in Toronto.

SHANNON CONWAY worked for the Economic Recovery Commission for one year and was a program presenter of "Getting the Message Out," an optimistic presentation on options for high school students in Newfoundland. She now works for a publishing company.

MURRAY COOLICAN is a former president of the Metropolitan Halifax Chamber of Commerce, and is currently the senior vice president of corporate resources at Maritime Life.

PARZIVAL COPES is professor emeritus at Simon Fraser University in Vancouver. He is the author of *St. John's and Newfoundland — An Economic Survey*, published in 1961.

MARCEL CÔTÉ is a political strategist and economist, and currently the CEO of Groupe Secor in Montreal. He was an advisor to former prime minister Brian Mulroney and former Quebec premier Robert Bourassa, and is the co-author, with David Johnston, of *If Quebec Goes* ....

DEANE CRABBE is the owner of H. J. Crabbe and Sons Mill, the sixth largest sawmill in New Brunswick. The company has been in business for more than 55 years.

JOHN CROSBIE has been involved in provincial and federal politics for 30 years. In the 1979 Clark government he was the minister of finance. In the Mulroney government he was justice minister and then minister of fisheries and oceans. It was Mr. Crosbie who announced the cod moratorium in his home province of Newfoundland.

BRIAN CROWLEY has been president of the Atlantic Provinces Council and a Dalhousie University professor of political science and economics. He is the author of *The Road to Equity*. He is also the founding president of the Atlantic Institute for Market Studies.

DOUG DAVIS is president of D. A. C. Davis Investment Counsel Inc. in Toronto.

PAUL DICK was an MP for 23 years, including eight years in Cabinet. He was the federal minister of supply and services from 1989 to 1993 and the Progressive Conservative deputy House leader in 1984. Trained as a lawyer, he was the assistant Crown attorney for the county of Carlton from 1969 to 1972.

JOHN DUVENAUD operates an information brokerage and management business in Winnipeg. He is an agriculture market analyst and the publisher of *Wild Oats Grain Market Advisory*.

KEN DYE was auditor general of Canada from 1981 to 1991.

DAVID FRAME is a former spokesperson for the Council of Ontario Construction Association in Toronto. He is now the director of the prevention branch at the Workplace Safety and Insurance Board, formerly the Workers' Compensation Board (WCB).

LLOYD FRANCIS was first elected to the House of Commons in 1963, where he served on and off for many years. He was named Speaker of the House in 1984 and was the Canadian ambassador to Portugal from 1984 to 1987.

CLAY GILSON, a former member of the U.S.–Canada Joint Commission on Grains, is professor emeritus of agricultural economics at the University of Manitoba.

WILF GOBERT, an oil industry investment analyst, is managing director of research for Peters & Co. Ltd. in Calgary.

TERRY GODSELL is the author of a 1982 report on Canadair/Bombardier. He is now retired.

JAY GORDON was an investment analyst specializing in the steel industry and is the former president of J. M. Gordon and Associates in Toronto. He is now retired.

JOHN ELDON GREEN spent 10 years as deputy minister of social services for the Prince Edward Island government and worked on economic development for the province. For the past 14 years he has been a management consultant in Charlottetown.

ROBERT GREENWOOD is a former director of the Economic Recovery Commission in St. John's and an adjunct professor with the Faculty of Business at Memorial University. He is currently a vice president of the Information Services Corporation of Saskatchewan.

MARK HALBERSTADT is the owner of Faster Linen Company in Toronto.

JIM HARRIMAN, former owner of Palliser Grain, is now a mortgage broker for the Invis Financial Group in Calgary.

RALPH HEDLIN is a veteran journalist and commentator. He is quoted extensively in Peter C. Newman's *Canadian Revolution*, especially in regard to Western discontent in Canada.

MAX HENDERSON trained as a chartered accountant and served on the Wartime Prices and Trade Board during the Second World War. He then worked for Samuel Bronfman in the private sector, but returned to government service as auditor general of Canada from 1960 to 1973. He died in December 1997.

RALPH HINDSON is a former director general of the materials branch of the federal Department of Industry, Trade and Commerce.s He is the author of the *Sydney Steel-Making Study*, released on October 2, 1967. In 1975 he was named the principal advisor on coal, iron, steel and related matters to Nova Scotia premier Gerald Regan.

JOHN HODGE was the senior vice-president of Montreal Shipping Inc. in Vancouver, British Columbia, at the time of his interview. He has since passed away.

HANK JENSEN is a former deputy commissioner of operations of the RCMP. He created the force's commercial crime branch.

ALLAN JOHNSTON is a grain broker and farmer in Welwyn, Saskatchewan.

GRAHAM KEDGLEY is president of his own consulting firm, KITAC Enterprises Ltd. in Vancouver, which specializes in international marketing, transportation, intergovernmental relations and finance. In 1970 he was director of marketing and later president of Neptune Bulk Terminals. In the early 1970s he was involved in the Grain Train, a successful bulk-grain transportation experiment to move grain more quickly and efficiently to port.

JASON KENNEY is a former president of the Canadian Taxpayers Association. He is now a Canadian Alliance MP representing Calgary Southeast. He is also the official Opposition's finance critic.

DIANE KEOUGH attended Memorial University in St. John's. She worked for the Economic Recovery Commission for one year and with Shannon Conway was a program presenter of "Getting the Message Out."

BARRY LACOMBE was the assistant deputy minister of verification, enforcement and compliance in the research branch of Revenue Canada in Ottawa until 1999. He is currently the president of the Canadian Steel Producers Association.

MONIQUE LANDRY was a Cabinet minister from 1986 to 1993. During that period she held the positions of minister for external relations and international development, secretary of state, minister of communications and minister designate of Canadian heritage.

BRUCE LEGGE, a retired major-general who spent 14 years working with disabled soldiers, was the chairman of the Workers' Compensation Board of Ontario from 1965 to 1973. He now practises law in Toronto.

KEITH LEWIS is a farmer from Wawota, Saskatchewan who sits on the board of governors of the Winnipeg Commodity Exchange. He is a former president of the Saskatchewan Canola Growers Association.

LES LIVERSIDGE is a management consultant in Toronto who helps guide businesses through the maze of regulations associated with workers' compensation. He is a member of the Employers' Council on Workers' Compensation.

TOM LIVINGSTON is a cattle farmer who lives on his ranch, Three Walking Sticks, on the banks of the Red Deer River near Duchess, Alberta.

MICHAEL MACDONALD is a former vice president of the Atlantic Canada Opportunities Agency (ACOA). He was in charge of the G7 summit in

Halifax in 1995 and headed Aird Associates, a consulting firm in Halifax, from 1991 to 1995. He then founded the Greater Halifax Partnership where he was CEO until 2001.

WILLIAM MACKNESS is a former senior vice president of Scotia McLeod and was vice president and chief economist with the Bank of Nova Scotia from 1982 to 1988. He was a senior advisor in the federal Department of Finance between 1966 and 1974, and an advisor to Finance Minister Michael Wilson in 1984. He was also dean of the Faculty of Management at the University of Manitoba. He is now retired.

STEVE MARSHALL was an articling law student when we met him.

PAUL MCCROSSAN is an actuary and partner in Eckler Partners Ltd., consulting actuaries in Don Mills, Ontario. He was an MP between 1978 and 1980, and again from 1984 to 1988, and served as parliamentary secretary to the minister of employment and immigration in 1979. McCrossan helped draft changes to the Canada Pension Plan in the mid-1980s.

CHARLIE MCMILLAN was the senior policy advisor to former prime minister Brian Mulroney from 1984 to 1987. He is now a professor of international business at York University in Toronto and chairman of Midas Capital Corporation.

TOM MCMILLAN, from Prince Edward Island, became an MP in 1979 and served as minister of tourism in 1984 and minister of the environment from 1985 to 1988. He was teaching in Boston at the time of his interview.

SEAN MOORE is the co-founder and former publisher of the *Lobby Monitor* and *Inside Ottawa*. He is now a public policy advisor with Gowlings, Strathy and Henderson, Barristers and Solicitors and Trade Mark Agents. He also is columnist with *The Hill Times*.

ROBERT NIELSEN, a native of New Brunswick, worked for *The Toronto Star* for 33 years, including a period as acting editor-in-chief. He now lives near Perth Andover, New Brunswick.

HARRY O'CONNELL worked in government in Prince Edward Island from the late 1970s to 1985. He was the deputy minister for the Department of Community Affairs, whose mandate was the revitalization of more than 30 communities in the province. He now owns his own computer retailing company.

Ron Olson, currently a financial consultant, was the vice president of Citibank Canada in the late 1980s.

Filip Palda is a professor of public administration at the École nationale d'administration publique in Hull, Quebec. He is also a senior fellow at the Fraser Institute.

Jim Pallister's family has been farming in Portage La Prairie, Manitoba, since 1898. He grows wheat and other crops on 4,400 acres and is a spokesperson for Farmers for Justice, a group battling the Canadian Wheat Board.

Arnie Patterson, a former press secretary to Pierre Trudeau, is a broadcaster and journalist living in Halifax. He has written a number of articles relating to the Sydney Steel Company in Sydney, Nova Scotia.

Marcel Pelletier had a 25-year career in the federal government, including positions as a law clerk, legal counsel to Parliament and advisor to new MPs of the rules, etiquette and traditions of Ottawa. After leaving the federal government he went to Haiti to advise the newly elected members on the responsibilities of democratic government. He is now a part-time professor at the University of Ottawa.

David Perry is a senior research associate with the Canadian Tax Foundation in Toronto.

Barry Prentice is a professional associate of the Transport Institute and an associate professor of agricultural economics and farm management at the University of Manitoba.

Steve Probyn is a former president of the Independent Power Producers' Society of Ontario and is currently president of Probyn and Associates in Toronto.

Gerard Protti has held several senior posts with the Alberta Energy and Treasury departments and has worked for the Canadian Energy Research Institute and Ontario Hydro. He is currently the senior vice president of Pan-Canadian Petroleum, in charge of new ventures.

FRED RANDLE is a farmer and rancher in High River, Alberta.

GORDON ROBERTSON joined the Department of External Affairs in 1941 and worked for every prime minister from Mackenzie King to Pierre Trudeau. He was clerk of the Privy Council and secretary to the Cabinet from 1963 to 1975 and was secretary to the Cabinet for federal-provincial relations from 1975 to 1979. He was also the principal constitutional advisor to prime ministers Lester Pearson and Pierre Trudeau. When he left the government he became president of the Institute for Research on Public Policy in Ottawa.

ALAN ROSS was the senior assistant deputy minister of supply and services from 1986 to 1993 and the director of financial policy for the comptroller general from 1973 to 1978.

DONALD SAVOIE wrote *The Politics of Public Spending in Canada*, the definitive book on the concept of spending in the Canadian political system. He is currently the senior fellow at the Institute for Research on Public Policy and holds the Clement-Cormier Chair in Economic Development at l'Université de Moncton in New Brunswick. From 1974 to 1982 he held various positions with the Department of Regional Economic Expansion and was also an advisor to prime ministers Mulroney and Chrétien. His latest book, *Governing from the Centre: The Concentration of Power in Canadian Politics*, is an assessment of the government of Jean Chrétien.

WALTER SCHROEDER is president and founder of the Dominion Bond Rating Service in Toronto.

DAVID SLATER was the general director of the federal Department of Finance from 1973 to 1978. He later ran the Economic Council of Canada.

JACK SLIBAR was a public policy and affairs counsel with the Public Policy Group at the time of his interview. He is now the executive director of the Toronto Humane Society.

JENNIFER SMITH formerly worked as a journalist with *The St. John's Telegram*. She is now a lawyer and works in the Supreme Court of Texas.

LARRY SOLOMON is the co-founder of Energy Probe Research Foundation in Toronto, an environmental and public policy research institute. He is the author of numerous books on public utilities, regulation, and public-private partnerships. He also writes a column for the *National Post*.

Rod Stamler, former head of the white collar crime unit of the RCMP, is a forensic accountant and a specialist on the underground economy. He resigned as assistant commissioner of the RCMP in 1989.

Catherine Swift is president of the Canadian Federation of Independent Business.

William Teron formerly served as chairman and president of the Canada Mortgage and Housing Corporation and headed a task force on the practice of a best-buy policy using public funds. He is now chairman of Teron International.

Kernaghan Webb is a senior legal policy analyst for consumer affairs at Industry Canada. He was a consultant on the study *Federal Government Relations with Interest Groups: A Reconsideration.*

Ron Whynacht is vice president and general manager of the National Sea Products processing plant in Lunenburg, Nova Scotia.

Stan Wilson was a cattle farmer who lived south of Chain Lakes in Alberta. He died on March 10, 2001.

Richard Wright is a past chairman of the Saskatchewan Pork Producers Marketing Board and is now president of Quadra Management Services in Outlook, Saskatchewan.

INTRODUCTION

Nineteen ninety-four was not a great year for Canada. The nation was coming out of a recession; unemployment was at near-record levels; taxes were the highest they had ever been; social programs were being cut; foreign investors were pulling their money out; and our dollar was falling like a rock.

At the same, time we were slowly seeing the emergence from the Ottawa woodwork of a large debt accumulated over a period that coincided approximately with our lifetimes. To many people the news just fell into the basket with all of the other financial problems facing the nation, but to the seven of us (without a degree in economics among us) the national debt was our initial focus.

When we started on this project our goal was to try to understand how, in less than 30 years, Canada had gone from being a debt-free country to one that owed $570 billion. Growing up, we hadn't been aware that the nation was running off the rails. But there we were at the end of 1994, recently out of university — where we were supposed to learn these things — asking, "Where the hell did this come from?"

The Team:
James Dungate, Vancouver, British Columbia
Kate Halpenny, Ottawa, Ontario
Jay Innes, Montreal, Quebec
Paul Kemp, Winnipeg, Manitoba
Thara Pillai, Edmonton, Alberta
Henk Van Leeuwen, Yarmouth, Nova Scotia
Moira Wright, Regina, Saskatchewan

One of the things that concerned me, and concerns me still, is that my generation has lived high on the hog and your generation's going to have to pay it off.

Gordon Robertson

PART ONE

GETTING HERE FROM THERE

CHAPTER 1

DEBT, DEPRESSION AND WAR

LOUIS BALTHAZAR
MAX HENDERSON
GORDON ROBERTSON

Soon after we began our travels across the country, we realized that the debt was just a symptom. But a symptom of what? As we began to look for the real cause of this economic slide, we knew that we would have to examine more than three decades of the country's history if we were to understand how our generation had been left with this overwhelming promissory note. So we asked people along the way to explain the Canada of our grandparents to us.

— The Team

What was the relationship between the provinces and the central government at the time of Confederation?

LOUIS BALTHAZAR

The original idea of Confederation was to form a unitary country. Yet, because Britain had given home rule to its colonies, we had a federation that was quite decentralized. Whenever the Judicial Committee of the Privy Council in London made judgments about the way powers were distributed, it tended to favour the provinces, so provinces were more autonomous than they are now.

In the 1930s three things happened. All of these developments tended to make Canada more of a unitary country and to give more power to the central government. In 1931, with the Statute of Westminster, Canada became fully sovereign in its foreign policy as well as its internal policy, and that created, I imagine, a feeling among the elites that at long last this country would be governed from its centre like most modern countries in the world. Then there was the economic crisis, which was very severe. And then we had the Second World War.

GORDON ROBERTSON

I don't think anybody who didn't live through the Depression can understand how it was, in magnitude an infinitely worse economic disaster than anything we've had since. But it was not only an economic disaster, it was a human disaster. Just to give you an idea, the levels of unemployment in Saskatchewan were 30, 40, 50 percent. It was similar in other parts of the country, although not as bad elsewhere as in Saskatchewan, Manitoba and Alberta. The only form of social security at the time was an old age pension introduced in 1927 for people 70 years and over. Twenty dollars a month. That was the only underwriting people had. There was nothing of any other kind whatsoever.

When the magnitude of the disaster became apparent and people were in desperate straits, it was the municipalities — not the provinces, not the federal government — that had to develop relief programs. And relief was handled in a very humiliating way. It was absolutely means tested and means tested in the most frugal, penny-pinching way because governments, too, were desperately hard up. Frugality was the order of the day because it had to be the order of the day. And then, of course, we got into the war.

LOUIS BALTHAZAR

At the beginning of the war the central government asked the provinces to give up their tax structures so that all income taxes would be concentrated for the war effort in the hands of the central government.

GORDON ROBERTSON

There are very few great things about war, but one of the great things here was the total unanimity of effort. There was some attempt on the part of Mr. Duplessis, the premier of Quebec, to create a difference between Quebec and the rest of the country, but that failed when he lost the election in 1940. Well, that finished it and Quebec rallied round so that you had complete unanimity.

We had to build up whole industries because Canada was an agricultural and resource-based country, not an industrial one. And the handling of finance by Canada during the war was superbly well done. C. D. Howe was one of the architects who changed our economy into an industrial wartime economy.[1] He brought to Ottawa, or to wherever they were required, people from all kinds of industry in Canada to make this conversion from peacetime to wartime and to build up the industries that were required for war. They were paid $1 a year.

MAX HENDERSON

We had several hundred of these administrators from industry helping the war effort. They were entitled to a cradle telephone, but if you were just an ordinary Joe who'd come to work for the government in the war, you had to have the old-fashioned kind, a stand-up telephone. If you were an administrator at $1 a year, you were expected to pay for your own lunches. That connoted that you were a wealthy man and therefore could afford to pay for lunches and take guests. These administrators could have a lower berth on the train. People the likes of me were only allowed $5 a day to live on. We had to take the upper berth on the train. If that wasn't being thrifty, I don't know what was.

The civil service during the Second World War had only about 45,000 employees to run the entire war economy. Today it's over 500,000.

GORDON ROBERTSON

It was a great time to be in the public service because everybody was working for the same goal. Canada was considered to have the best public service in the world. It was a superb public service.

When it became clear in 1944 that the war was going to end, planning began for post-war. There was a great determination that there must never again be the kind of economic and human situation we had experienced during the 1930s. And it's absolutely vital to understand that thinking, or you can't understand what was done after the war.

There was planning to ensure that there would not be an economic recession once the war was over. There was also a major increase in secondary and post-secondary education and financial assistance to universities because we were going to have a few hundred thousand men and women coming back, being demobilized from the services, and what were they going to do?

27

Then there was going to have to be some place to house people. So we had the new National Housing Act, and for the first time we had guaranteed mortgages so people with low incomes could hope to get mortgages at low interest to build houses. This produced not simply housing, but a construction industry.

It was also decided that some degree of social security was needed so the human suffering that occurred during the Depression would not recur. And out of that came a better old age pension, unemployment insurance and health insurance. All of these were planned and gradually implemented over the 1950s and into the 1960s. We were determined to get a social security net, but our determination was conditioned by the frugality of the pre-war period. It wasn't a sky-is-the-limit kind of thing. So the attitude toward post-war spending was conditioned by the need to avoid the economic letdown and unemployment that had occurred after the First World War. To the extent that spending was necessary to achieve these purposes, it was going to be done.

You've got to remember that during the war the country incurred an enormous burden of debt, but it was incurred for war purposes and we couldn't fight the war without borrowing. There was no way we could raise enough money through taxes. That debt was paid off after the war by budgetary surpluses that were created specifically to pay off that debt. In order to pay off debt — and this is not purely and simply economics, it's also politics — you have to have a conviction on the part of the populace that it's better to have a budgetary surplus, which means the government has more tax than it needs for immediate purposes in order to pay off the debt.

If during the war we had run up the kind of debt that we have now, what do you think would have been the reaction of the public?

GORDON ROBERTSON

We had a bigger debt! In 1946–7 it was 103 percent of GDP, compared to 66.9 percent in 1997–98.[2] But as I've said, it was incurred for war purposes, so there was no concern at all about borrowing to the hilt in order to fight the war. It was a quite different thing from our present situation. If there had been peace-time borrowing, there would certainly have been public concern.

A major effort was made, and it was successful, to pay off the wartime debt. It was run down almost totally, I think, in about 15 years after the war. The view was, of course, that debts have to be paid.

What was the atmosphere in the country after 1945?

GORDON ROBERTSON

Well, there was no recession and there was no significant amount of unemployment. Industry shifted from a wartime base to a peace-time one, many people achieved the kind of education they had missed during the war and the economy became remarkably prosperous. Canada was a leading industrial nation in the world at the time. Now, part of the reason we were doing so well was that a lot of the major industrial powers — Japan, Germany, France and so on — were on their backs. But envoys came from various countries to get our assistance and to establish trade relations. This was a demonstration of the success in the development of our economy, and this development was translated from wartime into peacetime. It was a very successful operation.

It seems that there was almost a euphoria coming out of the war.

GORDON ROBERTSON

Yes, euphoria's not too far off. It was a very good time to be Canadian. Indeed, Canadians had a sense of pride that I think has been equalled only in the first decade of this century when Sir Wilfrid Laurier said the 20th century belonged to Canada. Canada had done a first-class job in the war. There was post-war pride in the operation of our Armed Forces, pride in the operation of the economy and industry, and a good deal of pride in the post-war success in the swing back to peace. It was a very heady period.

NOTES

1. C. D. Howe moved from his position as minister of transport to become minister of munitions and supply in 1940. He was informally known as the "minister of everything" because of the number of posts he held during his political career.
2. GDP (gross domestic product) is calculated from the total value of goods and services produced within a nation's economy over a defined period.

CHAPTER 2

OTTAWA RISING

LOUIS BALTHAZAR
MARCEL CÔTÉ
MAX HENDERSON
BILL MACKNESS
GORDON ROBERTSON
DONALD SAVOIE

This was a Canada we knew little about and hardly recognized, but it was obviously a country that was strong and proud, with a secure and exciting future. We were slowly beginning to understand that the behaviour of the central government after the war resulted in a shift in the relationship between the provinces and Ottawa. This shift gradually altered the architecture and character of the nation, and it was into this "new" Canada that our generation was born.
— The Team

LOUIS BALTHAZAR

When the Second World War was over, the provinces — especially Quebec — thought they might regain some of the power they had had before the war. Yet Canada was reconstructing; Canada was becoming a middle power; there was a feeling that a modern Canada was being built. Most provinces accepted that the federal government would continue to play an important role.

Quebec was still reluctant, but it was reluctant in a passive way. Maurice Duplessis was back in power and he said, "The war is over. We want to control our taxes again." And he was successful in regaining some taxation power. He thought education could be served well by the religious communities. He thought the traditional institutions of Quebec could take care of social programs. All Duplessis could say was that we in Quebec would deal with our own things. He was against all federal programs but he had no alternatives. This is why we had to wait until the Quiet Revolution, until 1960, to see the full effect of Quebec's not accepting the new distribution of power.

For us in the 1950s in Quebec, everything that was progressive, that was good, that was modern, came from Ottawa. The provincial government had nothing to offer us.

Why didn't the federal government return those taxing powers to the provinces?

MARCEL CÔTÉ

Well, they found new uses for the money. They discovered unemployment insurance. They discovered free hospitalization and they discovered free university education. They discovered needs to be serviced, and decided to service them on a national basis.

Did other provinces resist?

MARCEL CÔTÉ

Not much, no. Quebec was the province that resisted the most. Ontario went along and the Western provinces went along, too. I guess all the premiers would have opposed Ottawa if they thought that their own people, their own electorate, would have backed them. Only in Quebec did the electorate back the provincial government. In the rest of Canada people more or less sided with the federal government, and the premiers decided to listen to the people.

Why was it so important for Quebec to retain those powers?

GORDON ROBERTSON

The provinces took different positions depending on their financial situations and the political complexion of their governments. The province of Quebec, not for financial reasons but for concern about the protection of its distinct culture and language, was more reluctant than any other province to see the federal government get into programs like social security, income support and health.

These things, the whole area of social security, strictly fall into provincial jurisdiction. And the only reason the federal government could get into them was that it can spend money on anything at all. It got into areas of provincial jurisdiction not because there was federal jurisdiction, because there wasn't, but because it could offer money.

DONALD SAVOIE

Since 1945 the feds have moved into every field of jurisdiction that moves and doesn't move. They've encroached all over the place.

MARCEL CÔTÉ

The health-care system, for example. Under the Constitution of Canada, the federal government has no power over health care. To gain control it made an agreement with the provinces that if the provinces would respect the federal government's restraints and run their health-care systems in a certain way, then they would be given money to manage their systems.

The federal government even built a highway, the Trans-Canada, in the 1950s. This was one of the biggest pork-barrel programs we've ever had in Canada. It was built by the federal government and the provinces, but under the leadership of the federal government. We built the road in the name of national unity and the voters bought it, I guess, because they didn't realize they were paying for it with their taxes!

DONALD SAVOIE

If there's one area of provincial jurisdiction, it's roads, but the feds are there building roads. If you look at the Constitution, the feds have no business in that. But they've been there. They've also been there in schools and hospitals. If the federal government would say tomorrow, "We are no longer willing to spend $1 in fields of provincial jurisdiction," you would have a totally different Canada ... in 12 months!

What was the effect of the gradual expansion of government as we moved into the 1960s?

DONALD SAVOIE

As the role of government expanded, it became much more complex. And as it became more complex, it became harder for the guardians to get a handle on spending. So as government grew, the guardians lost the edge.

Who are the guardians?

DONALD SAVOIE

In Ottawa it's the minister of finance and the president of the Treasury Board. Two guardians. It has been like that since day one and it's still like that. And against those two, all the rest, although up until 1945 it didn't matter. The role of the state was to run the post office, to have an army, provide some old age pensions perhaps, but that was essentially it. Parliament was simple and spending was simple. It mattered after 1945 because the role of the state became so wide-ranging.

When did the public begin to accept this growth in government?

DONALD SAVOIE

Well, attitudes changed in the 1960s. John F. Kennedy said in 1961 that by the end of the decade the United States would put a man on the moon. Hell of an objective! He turned to a government agency called NASA. Government was asked to put a man on the moon and government put a man on the moon. That's a hell of a thing back in 1961 to think that government could actually take a man from Earth, put him on the moon and bring him back safely. That was quite a goal, and it was met.

If we could do that, then people felt we could solve regional problems, urban decay, all kinds of things. So we had a decade or two when we had tremendous confidence in the ability of government to do whatever it set out to do. If, for example, we created a Department of Regional Economic Expansion, people on the East Coast said, "Well, good. We have an agency. If a government agency can put a man on the moon, surely an agency with a hundred million bucks can solve our problems." That was the mentality. That was the culture.

The politicians had buzz words and slogans — "Just Society" and "Great Society" — and people believed that government was the arm to change the world.[1]

BILL MACKNESS

Up to the late 1960s Canada had a worldwide reputation for financial rectitude. We went through the 1930s much better than the United States did. We kept our banks intact while the American banks went up in smoke. We developed world-class banking and insurance operations that operated worldwide. You don't get into that business if you have a reputation of being a financial village idiot. We had a wonderful reputation.

MAX HENDERSON

In the early 1960s MPs were very concerned about public waste. They were much more conscientious then. But that was when the proper thing to do was to handle public money as it should be handled. It was trust money. It was the money of the people. And when you're handling other people's money, you should be pretty careful what you do.

BILL MACKNESS

The average fiscal deficit in Canada between 1945 and 1955 was zero. Any small deficit was offset subsequently by small surpluses. We really were straight arrows. This gave us an exceptional financial sector and an extremely strong balance sheet.

DONALD SAVOIE

Things were booming in the late 1960s and this gave an open door to spenders to come in and do things.

BILL MACKNESS

Then someone found the balance sheet, and also found some lenders on Bay Street and Wall Street, and the party began!

NOTES

---

1. Pierre Trudeau talked about a "Just Society"; Lyndon B. Johnson spoke of a "Great Society."

CHAPTER 3

THE WAR BETWEEN THE WHIZ KIDS AND THE BEAN COUNTERS

PAUL DICK   ALAN ROSS
LLOYD FRANCIS   DAVID SLATER
MAX HENDERSON   ROD STAMLER
BILL MACKNESS   WILLIAM TERON

*A s we talked to people across the country, we heard more and
more about the changes in the late 1960s, and a clear picture
of the Canada into which we had been born began to emerge. At
a time when we were just learning to take our first faulty steps, the
government, hands deep in full pockets, head high and full of progressive ideas, was striding confidently into the future. But somewhere along the way it began to take some wrong turns.*

— The Team

When did the government begin to lose control of spending?

MAX HENDERSON

It started in 1963 with the implementation of the Glassco Royal
Commission on Government Organization. The government departments made thousands of recommendations to the commission, some
of them very good. But then the management consultants got in there.
Ottawa became the hottest place in Canada for management consultants. They came in and examined all the departments and made reports,
but the reports were generally written the way the head man of the
department wanted so that he could then go out and hire more staff,

increase the size of his office, get himself in line for a better promotion and of course send the bill to the treasury. This happened all over Ottawa. It was empire building at its best. That was when the explosion really occurred.

ALAN ROSS

I joined the government just after the Glassco Commission was established. Government had become so big that highly centralized control just wasn't working anymore, and there was a strong movement to bring in more modern management practices. That was the beginning of the philosophy, "Let the manager manage and get out of his face." That was the basic message behind Glassco.

The commission had a significant impact. Some of the major structural changes made were positive in that they overcame the stultifying effects of highly centralized control. But the major flaw that I see after all these years was that the government never replaced that control with an adequate accountability mechanism. It never found a way to make everybody truly responsible for the cost management of its programs.

When did the recommendations of the commission go into effect?

ALAN ROSS

The reforms for Glassco came in 1968 and 1969. But the reforms weren't in place for very long before someone realized that the government had taken away one set of controls and hadn't replaced it with another. By 1976 the auditor general said that the government had lost control, or was about to lose control. Now, in that milieu at that time, in the early 1970s, "control" was a very dirty word. You didn't use the word control in polite company.

Those were the years of free resources when we believed that the tax base could never get used up. There was revenue coming in; it was a growth time. As a matter of fact, it was almost as though money was a free good, and it's kind of hard to get people interested in accounting for money if it's a free good.

I think as well that the currency of the day for the major bureaucrats was ideas and new programs. That's what you got good marks for. Any idea was a good idea, and any program was a good program. It was an exciting time to be a politician because you were building new programs, you were building bridges, you were building monuments, you could do anything you wanted. And the philosophy of the managers was growth.

"I'm going to get promoted, I'm going to have more people reporting to me." The whole idea of accounting for your resources, of demonstrating your cost-management skills, just seemed to be redundant. The people who were in power considered discussions about program costs to be part of what they called the "bookkeeper mentality," and real managers didn't bother themselves with that kind of nonsense.

BILL MACKNESS

The generation of leaders from the 1970s forward was basically made up of people with no close experience of the disasters of the 1930s and therefore was less concerned with the cost management of government programs.

ALAN ROSS

The young officers who were recruited were smart and creative people, but they had no sense of the importance of the cost of a program. They felt sorry for people who didn't share this mentality because obviously we didn't have the same visionary skills, the same creative skills. We were restricted by this anal attitude, if you will. The senior mandarins of that time believed that anybody who was concerned with such things as costs and appropriate management was small-minded. "Think big," they said. "Think large. Let's not constrain ourselves with things like money. We'll look after that later. Or somebody will."

Whenever we raised cost issues at senior management committee meetings or down at the Treasury Board, there would be a laugh and someone would say, "Well, that's typical bean-counter mentality." The people on the rise were the economists and the political scientists, the policy people. There was a kind of love affair with policy. It was thought that these were the only people who could have a vision. If you were a bean counter, you couldn't have a vision.

PAUL DICK

Every time you have policy people in government, they dream up new policy, which means more expenditure of money. The term "whiz kids" has been used to describe a lot of the people who joined the public service in the early 1970s. A lot of them got tied into policy and they forgot to look at the dollars and cents.

Weren't there also significant changes in Parliament that allowed spending to get out of hand?

PAUL DICK

The principal change took place in 1969 when the government stopped doing the Estimates in the House of Commons in what was called the Committee of the Whole. It had been a way of slowing down government by tying up the Estimates for day after day. As a result, the government couldn't pass its legislation.

ALAN ROSS

When the Estimates were discussed in the Committee of the Whole in the House of Commons, the whole House reserved the right to scrutinize a department's estimates. But through parliamentary reform, the House lost that particular facility and as a result lost some of its control.

PAUL DICK

In the first year of the Trudeau administration they changed the rules of the House of Commons by invoking closure and moved the Estimates into committees outside the House — the standing committees. The committee members could discuss the Estimates and vote on them, but the rules were changed so that if they did not vote on them by the 15th of June, then the Estimates would be deemed to have passed. Well, as soon as the Estimates were deemed to have passed, everybody lost interest in them. As a result, the committee members started to argue about policy at the standing committees. They no longer discussed the finances of a department. Nobody was counting the beans anymore. Nobody was taking a look at what was happening with the dollars and cents. That's when we lost public scrutiny of Parliament.

ALAN ROSS

And I think that until we reform parliamentary committees to allow visibility and the exposure of the Estimates that can't be managed by the bureaucracy, the situation will continue.

Wasn't there anyone in government whose job was to control spending?

ROD STAMLER

Yes, but late in the 1960s the Office of the Comptroller General was practically eliminated and the spending authority was given to the ministers. Prior to that, budgets had to be religiously followed. The comptroller general reported to Parliament and was responsible for the budgets. He was the person who said, "No, you can't spend that. No, you can't build that facility this year because it wasn't planned for." In those days he had an overriding authority.

Now, although the position still exists, it has no power. Now the auditor general looks at the money after it's spent and reports on how departments misspent their budgets. But the task of looking at the money before it is spent — that job has been given to the politicians at large.

When a politician has a multimillion-dollar project he wants to develop, who does he go to for approval?

ROD STAMLER

He goes to the Treasury Board for approval, and since the Treasury Board is headed by one of the ministers of Cabinet, he is actually going to another politician. It's a circular process. If Cabinet decides that it's good to have the requested facility, then it's likely the Treasury Board will authorize that expenditure. Whereas if you go back to the comptroller general era, that facility would have had to have been planned, budgeted for and approved, perhaps years in advance of its being built.

DAVID SLATER

When I was in the Department of Finance, we used to say that in a Cabinet of 27 ministers there were 25 spending ministers, a prime minister and one anti-spending minister. The one anti-spending minister was the minister of finance, and the perpetual job of the Department of Finance and the Treasury Board was to try to beat off the incredible pressure of the spending ministers and the caucus, all of whom wanted to get things for their "good works." And it's very difficult to appreciate how enormous and how subtle and how complex the pressure is that is imposed from across the country on spending ministers.

The best illustration of this spending pressure occurred about February every year, when there would be something called the fiscal framework established to go through Cabinet. And that framework for the year would have in it a certain amount of reserve money. But two or three years running, all those reserves were committed before the fiscal year even started. The spenders had gotten to the prime minister, and if the prime minister was soft, the finance minister couldn't stop the spenders. You've got to have a prime minister with sufficient control over his

Cabinet and his caucus to say, "No." But prime ministers don't always have that power or don't choose to use it.

LLOYD FRANCIS

Looking back, there were some easy years in the 1970s when revenues rolled in. We even had periods of surpluses. Hard to believe. When there's a surplus and the country is prosperous and revenues are high, there are always proposals for spending. And this is when the discipline that had prevailed disappeared. At times of great optimism it seems that the future will be just like the past. Well, it isn't.

WILLIAM TERON

In the early and mid-1970s the government had a lot of good intentions and everybody thought they could do great things. Ministers and Cabinet were eager for ideas, and if a good idea came forward, the government virtually jumped at the great opportunity to do good. At the time they honestly felt that they were doing good, and they were, in the short run.

I don't think any of them actually saw that there was an end to the rainbow.

CHAPTER 4

GOOD TIMES
AND GREAT EXPECTATIONS

MARCEL CÔTÉ
BRIAN CROWLEY
PAUL MCCROSSAN
FILIP PALDA
ALAN ROSS
WILLIAM TERON

Gordon Robertson described the years after the war, the late 1940s, as being a "heady" time for Canada. The late 1960s turned out to be another heady time for the country. Expo 67 in Montreal was a phenomenal international success, and the city was preparing to host the Olympic summer games. Flower power was replaced by Trudeaumania when Pierre Elliot Trudeau became our 15th prime minister in 1968. People prospered and became accustomed to the good life. The country was united, proud and, apparently, rich. Our parents' generation, basking in the reflected glory of Canada's success on the international stage and enjoying our new and seemingly endless prosperity, believed that it had demonstrated its full support for the government and could now expect something in return.

— The Team

PAUL MCCROSSAN

The predominant social ethic of the 1960s and 1970s was to help out the less fortunate, and people thought that since we were a rich country with all the resources that we could ever need, we could never have debt problems.

At the time Parliament saw its job as sharing the wealth. To protect Canadians against the costs of diseases that were going to catch up with them sooner or later, Parliament brought in medicare. To protect senior citizens through old age, it brought in the Canada Pension Plan. There were so many problems to be dealt with, but we were a very rich society with no debts. It was a question of "Let's share the wealth and help the less wealthy."

But then we started spending more than we were collecting. In 1972 the budget was essentially balanced. During 1973 and 1974 we started to have our first deficits. They weren't very big. From 1974 to 1979 they increased from a couple of billion to $10 billion a year. That was cause for alarm.

ALAN ROSS

We began to think that since we were into a growth mode and would have a larger population tomorrow, we'd be able to spread the cost over more people and could therefore afford these big programs. We deluded ourselves.

WILLIAM TERON

And it wasn't just the politicians. The public started to have these great expectations and they fuelled the demands.

ALAN ROSS

Collectively we became more demanding. We had a whole generation of Canadians who drove politicians, who had great expectations, who insisted that government become more involved in the issues of Canadians, whether these issues were grants to business, subsidies or immigration. There was an acceptance by the public, generally, that government was going to look after them.

How did Canadians get involved in the growth of the late 1960s, and what changed in our relationship with the government?

BRIAN CROWLEY

There are basically two ways that people can make themselves better off. They can either make wealth or they can take wealth. To make wealth you offer a good or service that people buy voluntarily. You offer your service, and somebody comes along and says, "I want that, here's some money for it." Everybody is made better off by that transaction. The buyer would rather have the service you provide than the money that he or she had. That's making productivity. That's making economic wealth.

Taking, on the other hand, involves some agency stepping in and saying, "You have something, but I think this other person over there should have it so I'm taking it from you and giving it to them. OK?" That's taking.

Now, the government plays a huge redistributive role in society. They are the principal agency of taking, as opposed to making. What's happened is that as the size of government has grown, more and more of us — and, believe me, every one of us is involved — have become part of the taking activity. We all receive some good or service from government that is subsidized by the taxpayers. People who are at university, people who watch the CBC, we're all involved. More and more people have developed an interest in the activity of taking rather than the activity of making.

Almost everything the government does involves some element of redistribution. For example, unemployment insurance is a system in which employees who are rarely laid off, who rarely need unemployment insurance, transfer part of their wealth to workers who are frequently laid off or are seasonal workers. But it's not just workers who are making that transfer. Employers are also subsidizing other employers whose labour costs would otherwise be higher.

FILIP PALDA

If you passed through the university system, then you've also benefited. Most people don't know that university costs 10 times as much to the government as a student pays in tuition. The rest is being picked up by the taxpayers.

MARCEL CÔTÉ

One of the reasons to redistribute is to make sure that the "have-not" provinces receive the same level of service as the "have" provinces. The problem is that we tax $300 billion and redistribute only about $20 billion. The rest just goes to Ottawa and then goes back to the provinces in the form of transfer payments. We seem to be taxing a lot for the amount of redistribution we're doing.

BRIAN CROWLEY

The problem with this system is that it creates huge, powerful vested interests that are in favour of the system as it exists. The more money that is transferred to people through government, the more people there will be within society who have an interest in keeping government large and active, with its fingers in various parts of the economy.

Back when government handled only 20 or 25 percent of the gross domestic product, people didn't spend a lot of time thinking about how they could get extra benefits out of government. They had to put their efforts into the private economy, into finding goods and services that people actually wanted to buy. Now, however, almost half of the value of the economy is passing through government's hands, and people see that it's in their interest to spend a lot more time putting their energies into taking rather than into making. And when you consider that in the vast majority of cases economic growth flows from innovation, from change and from transferring resources from one use to another where they're more productive, this behaviour is a huge drag on the economy and something that we have not begun to come to terms with.

How difficult is it to get money from government?

BRIAN CROWLEY

It's very easy to get benefits out of government. It's very easy for groups to organize and ask for a specific benefit, whether it's a tariff or a wage subsidy or a subsidy to investment or whatever. It's very hard, however, for government to stop paying a benefit once it has started because paying a benefit creates a group with an interest in keeping that benefit, and they will lobby till the cows come home in order to defend that interest. If you were getting, say, a $10,000 subsidy every year, it would be worth your while to pay $9,000 a year to defend it because you'd still be $1,000 a year better off. But if I'm paying, through my taxes, $1 a year toward that subsidy, the interest I have in organizing to end that subsidy is tiny. But the incentive you have to fight to keep it is huge.

FILIP PALDA

But what these people don't see directly, and what they might not feel so good about if they understood it, is that the grant is being sucked away from another productive part of the economy. It is knocking people out of work somewhere else.

The system is so big and so complicated now that we can't understand the full consequences of our actions.

CHAPTER 5

SHERPAS AND HIRED GUNS

CHARLIE MCMILLAN
SEAN MOORE
FILIP PALDA
DONALD SAVOIE
JACK SLIBAR
KERNAGHAN WEBB

A s people of our parents' generation began getting more from government, they quite naturally demanded more from government and organized themselves into groups to make sure their demands were heard on Parliament Hill. Special-interest groups blossomed and spread across the country like ragweed.

Young people today might find it easy to pass judgment on our parents because we've been left holding the bag. But can we truthfully say that we wouldn't have been interested in getting our share out of government too? Wouldn't we have fallen into the same trap? After all, the money was there for the taking. Can we honestly say, now that we're adults, that we haven't been guilty of lobbying the government for something? We were beginning to learn that fingers can point in more than one direction.

— The Team

KERNAGHAN WEBB

After the war, the government started establishing more and more socially oriented programs, assisting various disadvantaged groups and trying to address more and more problems. There came to be, I wouldn't want to call it a shadow government, but a parallel group of concerned individuals clustering around each regulatory regime, all with their own particular perspective on how the law was being applied or how the law could be changed. As government grew, so did the belief that government could do more than it had before and solve many of society's problems.

SEAN MOORE

In Canada there have been lobbyists right from the beginning of the parliamentary system. Some of the scandals associated with the building of the railway were instances of perhaps overzealous lobbying by railway interests who were trying to influence the decisions of the government of the day about where railways were going to go and under what terms they would be built. We've always had lobbyists.

However, interest groups have probably taken on more prominence in the last 15 or 20 years because of increased media scrutiny and because the nature of our decision making has changed. In this country we used to have a system of what was called "elite accommodation," where a lot of important decisions were made quietly behind closed doors. These days the nature of the elites has changed. The leaders of interest groups have become in some respects part of the elite in Canada.

It's increasingly difficult for government to make decisions without being able to demonstrate that whatever it is it's deciding is generally in the public interest.

KERNAGHAN WEBB

It's standard practice to say that whatever position your group is advocating will be in the best interests of society in general. This led us to the conclusion that the term "public interest" has been inflated by so many people, using it in so many contexts, that it is essentially meaningless.

SEAN MOORE

We belong to all sorts of interest groups whether we know it or not. If you take out a membership in the Canadian Automobile Association for their tow truck service, then all of a sudden you're a member of the CAA and its lobby against higher gas prices.

JACK SLIBAR

The thing we have to realize is that everybody, absolutely everybody, is a lobbyist to one degree or another. If you're a student, you have interests that particular associations are advocating. If you're a housewife, if you're a consumer, it doesn't matter what you do, there is probably an organization that is representing, to a greater or lesser degree, your particular views.

Sean Moore

Society is increasingly being organized on this interest-group basis. One of the things that is frustrating is that we have this cacophony of voices in society, all of whom are saying, "I'm different, I deserve special treatment." I believe many Canadians are asking themselves, "Don't we have anything in common?" However, if we want to have a democratic system that takes into account the legitimate interests of a wide range of groups in society, we have to accept these differ-ent voices. Governments are well aware of this as we continue to have this orgy of consultation. You often have to sit there and lis-ten to people who don't know what the hell they're talking about. But they have a right to their particular views. Democracy's messy. Democracy's noisy.

Filip Palda

There are so many interest groups because so much is up for grabs. In the days of the settlers there were lots of buffalo grazing on the plains of North America. Word got around and all of sudden you had Buffalo Bill and God knows how many hordes taking potshots and bagging 20 buf-falo just to have their pictures taken with them — all because the buffa-lo were there for the taking. Now government is there for the taking. It's like an open plain and the resources that are grazing there are the resources of the economy.

Donald Savoie

We've reached a point in this country, as the Americans did much earlier, where government is so complex that it takes a professional to know how it works. You need expertise to make sense of Ottawa.

What exactly does a lobbyist do?

Jack Slibar

In a pluralistic society everyone has a right to be heard, and I'm simply a hired gun. When an organization comes to me and says that it wants to advocate a particular view to government officials, or members of the bureaucracy, or to the opposition parties, it's my job to be unbiased, to look at the policy they're advocating and find the best way to present it to the appropriate group within the system.

My purpose is to provide associations or other groups with an advocacy role. What I attempt to do is to package the association's wants and desires in such a way that they're understandable from the standpoint of government and that they're packaged correctly to conform with the objectives of the department that the association is trying to lobby.

Most people think that lobbyists go to government and have a secret lunch in the backroom of a hotel or a private club, a bag of money changes hands and somebody suddenly gets a contract. It really doesn't work that way. Most lobbying — I would say 70 percent in Canada — is done at the bureaucratic or administrative level. Only about 30 percent is done in the legislative arena. The bureaucracy, in general, develops policy, whereas the legislature or the Commons or Parliament enacts laws.

KERNAGHAN WEBB

Ultimately the choice is usually made by an individual bureaucrat operating with the full knowledge and authority of his or her minister. The bureaucrat is the one who points the finger and says, "You're a winner; you're a loser. We're going to give you some money, but we're not going to give you any."

JACK SLIBAR

Remember, there isn't only one interest group at the table for any particular policy issue. There might be hundreds, even thousands, of potential associations or groups interested in that topic. As a result, government has a system set up to listen to what these various associations are saying.

Who does the government listen to?

JACK SLIBAR

If a very powerful, well-established association is advocating a particular policy and the government offends that group, then the government has to be concerned about votes in the next election. If it's an industry association, one has to be concerned that the group might pick up and leave the province or the country if it is rejected, in which case jobs are lost, tax revenue is lost, and spinoff industries will be lost. All of these things factor into how much a group is listened to.

48

If I were involved in a small association, without a lot of savvy in the lobbying area, could I have an impact?

JACK SLIBAR

If you were a small association that was ignorant about how government functions, you would have a very difficult time advocating a particular policy because you wouldn't know where to advocate your particular views. What you would need is a Sherpa. You need someone to take you by the hand and guide you through the process.

So you're my guide?

JACK SLIBAR

I'm your Sherpa.

CHARLIE MCMILLAN

The business of interest groups and lobbyists is another insidious process that feeds the various spending patterns of government. It's a self-re-enforcing cycle. The whole damn thing should have been dismantled long ago. It's another vote-buying exercise. Ministry after ministry has been throwing money at people in the name of consultation. In effect it's appeasement. It's to buy off their voices.

The reality is that, in Ottawa in particular, consultation is the simple form of indecision. Part of the problem of the Mulroney government was that when they should have consulted, they acted and when they should have acted, they consulted because they couldn't make up their minds.

FILIP PALDA

There are a lot of talented people in these interest groups who devote their lives to milking government. Instead of finding productive uses in the economy and making the pie bigger, they're a section of the economy that is trying to cut the pie up. When there is too much pie-cutting, the economy starts to shrink rapidly. This is the problem with a lot of underdeveloped countries: the best people are in the pie-cutting, not the pie-baking, business.

SEAN MOORE

I don't think you need lobbyists or government relations consultants to be effective in public policy advocacy if you take the time to learn how decisions are being made and what the factors are that are most important in the minds of decision makers. Many Canadians generally, and interest groups in particular, don't take the time to understand how these decisions are made. As a result they get frustrated and think there's some kind of magic potion that a lobbyist is going to give them.

It's not rocket science these guys are involved in. It's tracking the personal politics and the dynamics of decision making in a complex government. Unfortunately our educational system is not very good at teaching that. What we need is some real political education in Canada that explains how decisions are made and how people can play a real role in the system. To assume that on a wide variety of issues MPs and Parliament are the real decision-making authorities in Canada is not a very good place to start.

PART TWO

GRABBING WITH BOTH HANDS

CHAPTER 6

R.I.P. SYDNEY STEEL

BRIAN CROWLEY   ARNIE PATTERSON
JAY GORDON   DONALD SAVOIE
RALPH HINDSON   CATHERINE SWIFT
CHARLIE MCMILLAN

Our visit to Sydney, Nova Scotia, left a lasting impression on us all. Though we'd been told that the autumn weather in Cape Breton was glorious, a heavy rain fell during our drive to the Sydney Steel Company (SYSCO) plant. The grey October skies seemed an appropriate setting for our look into the industry that was once the heart of this town. We wondered whether the sun had surrendered to the "Danger: Keep Away" signs that guarded the tar ponds bordering the plant.

Across the street from these deadly pools, which won't be cleaned up for many years to come, was a house decorated quite spectacularly for Halloween. Orange and black crepe paper was strung above the open porch, witches flew, ghosts and skeletons floated and shook in the cold wind. Appropriately, in the centre of the yard was a large Styrofoam tombstone and carved below a skull and crossbones were the letters "R.I.P."

— The Team

DONALD SAVOIE

I think in many instances the private sector has been a complete fraud. Businesspeople will fly to Ottawa and argue to cut spending, but they'll be the first at the trough, grabbing with both hands.

CATHERINE SWIFT

There are program junkies in business, just as there are program junkies anywhere. And once they become dependent they need their fix every now and again. In a climate and culture that promotes subsidies to businesses, you have "grantrepreneurs," people who are accomplished at getting grants. They're not particularly good at running a business, but they're very good at getting grants. As long as they happen to be in the right minister's riding, or are in the industry that's the flavour of the month for government, they can get millions and millions of dollars.

CHARLIE McMILLAN

Companies are into government for money all the time. It's part and parcel of the process and it occurs in insidious ways. Companies get to their local MP. The MP gets to the regional Cabinet minister. A head of steam builds up and eventually the request reaches the Cabinet or the bureaucrats. You have this snowball effect and everybody's saying, "Well, how do we address this 'political' issue?" It goes back to the old definition of politics: who gets what? Who, what, where?

And once other companies know that there is a pot of money there to be had, they get in on it too, for competitive advantage. If one company is going after the money, then another company has to get it as well. And that shows just how insidious the whole process is.

CATHERINE SWIFT

Subsidies tend to be motivated by a politician wanting to hand over a cheque and shake somebody's hand in front of some media cameras. They tend to be motivated by pork barrelling so the politician can get re-elected next time around. Subsidies are rarely, if ever, motivated by good, sound economic reasons. The resource sector, like the steel industry, is full of instances where billions and billions of dollars have been thrown into sinkholes.

CHARLIE McMILLAN

The real form of wealth creation for a century has been in our raw materials. We dig the minerals out of the ground, we sell the forest, we sell the fish. We flog these resources to the United States and around the world.

But that wealth is no longer there. We've overfished. We haven't managed our forestry. We haven't managed our mining.

But if you look at Japan or the United States — at Hollywood or at California's Silicon Valley — you will see new forms of wealth tied to innovation. People don't need our raw materials the way they did a century ago.

BRIAN CROWLEY

The more we strive to protect our established way of doing things, our established industries, the more we freeze out innovation, the source of economic growth, and the more we prevent the economy from evolving naturally over the years. When we pay subsidies to industries that are not economical, that don't make a profit, that have lost their markets, we just put off the day when we all have to recognize that people can't be protected from the changes that are going on in the world.

CHARLIE MCMILLAN

And Ottawa's missing the point. The confusion and the inefficiencies in government reflect a much bigger process. Government can no longer do the things it could a generation ago. Governments can't deliver the way they used to. The wealth-creation process is no longer in government or in the public sector. It's tied to technology. It's tied to small businesses. It's tied to the innovative process. Governments are totally ignorant about the whole exercise.

Some people have been trying to turn back the clock and use government as a protective device, as a prop. As a result, companies and industries are dependent on the tax system to prop things up.

The Sydney Steel Corporation[1]

JAY GORDON

I don't think there's a steel producer in North America who hasn't had his hand in the pot to at least some degree. What is interesting in the Canadian experience is that the companies that have been the greatest beneficiaries of government largesse have been the greatest flops. The most egregious example is Sydney Steel (SYSCO) in Sydney, Nova Scotia.

Since they took it over the provincial and federal governments have poured more than $2 billion into SYSCO. Today [1995] SYSCO doesn't use either coal or iron ore. It's based on scrap. When you're only producing a quarter of a million tons of rails a year you don't need a hell of a lot of scrap.

Essentially what SYSCO proves is that you cannot save jobs that don't have an economic raison d'être. It's that simple.

When was the steel industry established in Cape Breton?

ARNIE PATTERSON

The Dominion Steel and Coal Corporation (DOSCO) was founded in Cape Breton, at the beginning of the century. At that time the steel industry made great sense at this location because Sydney was on tide water and the major markets for steel were in Europe. There was coal in Cape Breton and there was iron ore in Pictou County and in nearby Newfoundland. Most of the money that went into that development in 1900 was British money. In fact, the company was first known as the British Empire Steel and Coal Corporation (BESCO). At one time BESCO, and later DOSCO, had more than 20,000 employees.

The company was relatively prosperous but it always needed government support.

RALPH HINDSON

At the end of the last century it was the world view in the industry that steel-making plants should be built as close as possible to raw materials. In those days they used a great deal more iron ore and a great deal more coking coal to produce a ton of steel than plants do today. I'm talking about the 1890s.

Technology then changed. Less coal and higher-grade ores were needed and since the ore from Wabana in Newfoundland was not of a very high quality, the plant at Sydney was obsolete the day it was built.

ARNIE PATTERSON

SYSCO was formed after 1967 when Hawker Siddeley, the company that owned DOSCO, decided to close the steel plant. They were faced with a massive capital expenditure to improve and modernize the plant and they opted not to do so. The plant was losing money and they thought they would never get the capital back. Then the provincial government stepped in.

Ralph Hindson

Two years before the province took it over I instigated the *Sydney Steel-Making Study* in my capacity as general director of the materials branch, the part of the federal government responsible for the steel industry. The study, which was published in October of 1967, clearly showed that the company had no real future, mainly because of its distance from its markets. It showed the high cost of production, the high cost of producing steel, the high cost of rolling steel. It was a very negative report.

Was this the first report of its kind?

Ralph Hindson

No, no. It was about the fifth or sixth — all of the others showing the same thing over the years.

Three weeks after the study came out DOSCO announced it was closing Sydney Steel. The people in Nova Scotia were shocked and all hell broke loose because SYSCO was the major employer in the province. Ike Smith was the interim premier because Robert Stanfield was on the hustings in the leadership campaign for the Conservative Party. Smith's Cabinet met with Arthur G. McKee and Company, a group of well-known American consultants on the iron and steel industry. The Americans clearly advised the Government of Nova Scotia not to take over the steel plant. It was not viable and never would be. Their report stressed the distance from markets. The plant was more than 1,000 miles from its principal market, whereas other steel companies were only 100 or 200 miles away from their major markets. It was a very good report.

I might add that the same company had done a report on the steel industry in Cape Breton in 1944 in which the same things were said, and that report was ignored, just as their report in 1967 was ignored.

Arnie Patterson

The unions were of course militant in wanting the government to take over the steel plant. It had been the major muscle in the Cape Breton economy for 67 years. It involved thousands and thousands of people and their dependants and the government thought that they could probably run it better. The takeover was also a social measure; one, unfortunately, that didn't work that well.

RALPH HINDSON

When you have a situation where the church, the unions, the merchants and the steel-plant workers form a monolithic group that collectively has great force and puts pressure on the government, you have a fair amount of political clout that is closely identified with certain politicians, and the politicians directly involved get even more involved.

JAY GORDON

The people we elect to govern us have no conception of what they're doing from an economic point of view, or for that matter from a social point of view. After all, if you screw up the economy, you're screwing up the society.

ARNIE PATTERSON

If the SYSCO plant in Sydney were in Wheeling, West Virginia, it would have been closed 25 years ago because the Americans make those decisions on the basis of a profit-and-loss statement. We're a little slower to arrive at those decisions because we deal with them on a political basis, and we deal with them on the basis of social welfare.

RALPH HINDSON

Sydney Steel got into very serious trouble again in 1974 and 1975 because after the Government of Nova Scotia took it over, the people running SYSCO made a big hullabaloo about how successful they were. Their views were greatly exaggerated, but they persuaded the government to allow them to put in the neighbourhood of $125 million into modernizing the plant. That was a big mistake because it contributed greatly to the future problems. The company couldn't make enough money out of that expenditure to even pay the interest on the loan, and the debt has hung over Sydney Steel's head ever since.

JAY GORDON

In the early 1990s the facilities at SYSCO were upgraded and the company switched to an electric furnace operation at a cost of more than $200 million. The government also subsidized SYSCO's so-called sales. A major portion of the company's sales over the years have been to countries like Bangladesh, which never had any hope in hell of ever paying the money back. Every time Bangladesh would get hit by another typhoon or hurricane or what have you, Mr. Clark, when he was minister for external affairs, would stand up in Ottawa and say something like, "Our poor friends in Bangladesh have been hit by another natural disaster, so we're going to forget that we shipped them 25,000 tons of rails last week, and we're not going to make them pay for them."[2]

And I really don't feel obliged to subsidize Mexico City's wonderful new subway. That's what we've been doing. Who's subsidizing my subway? We're building an extension in Toronto and it's going to cost hundreds of millions of dollars but we're not getting any rails from Bangladesh or Mexico or anywhere else. We're going to have to pay for them.

RALPH HINDSON

When you think of the amount of money that's been spent on SYSCO since the day it was taken over! If that money had been more properly used in Nova Scotia, what a difference that would have made. I calculated that we could send every Sydney Steel employee to Florida, give them each $20,000 and we'd still save money.

Companies have a right to die too, you know. And I don't think politicians should be allowed to get involved in giving them grants and large subsidies.

JAY GORDON

But the biggest cost of SYSCO is not the money that has been thrown away to keep a handful of people working in Sydney, Nova Scotia. The biggest cost is that in the process they created the centrepiece of downtown Sydney — the tar ponds! These people have literally been killing themselves and their children by drinking water that's been contaminated by the tar ponds and by breathing air that's been contaminated. The real costs of the SYSCO experiment are just beginning to be felt as people wind up in hospital with emphysema, lung cancer and all sorts of incurable diseases.

That's not only counterproductive, it's the ultimate form of stupidity.

NOTES

---

1. A Short History of SYSCO:
   Before the Sydney Steel plant closed early in 2001, it consisted of two blast furnaces and several basic open-hearth furnaces, with an

annual raw steel capacity of about 910,000 tonnes. It produced rails and semi-finished steel. In 30 years more than $2.8 billion of taxpayers' money has been spent on SYSCO.

1899	BESCO (later DOSCO) is founded to exploit Cape Breton coal and Newfoundland iron ore.
1905	Plant starts production of railway rails.
1960	Hawker Siddeley takes over the plant.
1967	Province of Nova Scotia establishes a Crown corporation to keep the industry alive and buys the plant for $50 million, renaming it SYSCO.
1987	Federal government approves $275 million to modernize the mill, including the installation of an electric-arc furnace.
1994	Half-interest in the plant is sold to a Chinese firm, Minmetals.
1997	In December Minmetals, who never invested any money in the plant, declines its option to buy.
1993–1998	Liberal government in Ottawa promises twice to stop funding the mill but reneges both times after attempts to privatize the plant fail.
1998	A plan to sell Sydney Steel to a Mexican company for U.S. $26 million fails.
1998	Nova Scotia government brings in the Dutch steel maker Hoogovens to manage the mill and find a buyer. Hoogovens is the fourth potential buyer since the province put it up for sale in 1992.
1998	The province sets a January 1 deadline to sell the steel mill, but the deadline passes without a deal. In March the Nova Scotia government debates further bailouts to SYSCO.
2001	The plant closes and in late August the assets are auctioned off.

2. Joe Clark was the minister of external affairs from 1984 to 1991.

CHAPTER 7

BAILOUT

TERRY GODSELL
RON OLSON

We found a photograph of the sod turning when construction began on the magnesium plant in High River, Alberta. There's a row of politicians in hardhats, all smiles and leaning on shovels. There, near the end of the row, is Ralph Klein. Back in the late 1980s he was the energy minister who gave the thumbs-up to the loan guarantee that would pay for three-quarters of the cost of building the plant.[1] That's the same Ralph Klein who is now the premier of Alberta.

Six years later we rolled over the same ground. We seemed to be in the middle of nowhere, corralled by fields on one side and foothills on the other, a highway with little traffic somewhere in the distance. The magnesium plant was now a modern-day ruin. Seeing all the boxes and equipment piled inside the fence, a stranger might have thought the workers were just away on a break, but the only employee on the site was a lonely security guard.

— The Team

The High River Magnesium Plant[2]

RON OLSON

In late 1987 when I was vice president of Citibank, Alberta Natural Gas asked Citibank and a number of other banks to put together financing proposals for the construction of a magnesium plant. We put in our proposal and along with the Royal Bank of Canada were selected to lend money for the plant.

Now, banks are in the business of obtaining money from people who have surplus funds and lending that money to people who require funds. Banks try to find investments that are risk free, and whenever a bank makes a loan, it tries to make sure that it has at least two ways out of the loan. In this case, if the plant was successful, the banks would get their money back from operations and profits. If it wasn't, the bank had a government guarantee from the province of Alberta. So since there were relatively few financial risks, the loan was judged to be acceptable from a banker's perspective.

At the time the Alberta government was interested in diversifying the province's economic base. If this plant had worked, there would have been a lot of secondary industry established in this area. There was great incentive for the province to backstop the plant, and people at various levels of government felt that they should be more involved in managing the capital in industry, as opposed to allowing the private sector to take care of these matters. Without government guarantees this plant would not have gone ahead because there was only one company, Alberta Natural Gas, willing to put up any equity, but they limited their contribution to one-quarter of the capital costs.

What kind of money are we talking about?

RON OLSON

The plant operated from the initial start-up for probably a year or a year and a half and then it closed because of low magnesium prices. It cost approximately $130 million to $135 million up to the time it started operations. From that time on there was probably another $40 million put into the plant and its mothballing by Alberta Natural Gas. So we have a total in the area of $175 million, of which the government guaranteed the first $102 million. In addition, the province has been funding interest on the loan since 1990, and that runs in the neighbourhood of $10 million a year. Essentially $175 million has been lost.

If the money hadn't gone into that project, it would have been available for other economic activities that the government still needs to fund. For example, we've got a highway being built a short distance away from here in High River. The government is paying for that highway with new funds. It could have used the money that has been going to pay the interest on this loan to build that highway.

The essential lesson to be learned here is that no matter how attractive it looks, or what the rationale for government involvement, if the private sector is not willing to put up all of the capital for ventures such as this, the government should stay away. Politicians and people who work for the government who make decisions of this nature are not held accountable as in private industry. In private industry, if you bankrupt your company, you've lost all of the shareholders' capital and the company goes out of business. When governments get involved in capital projects like this that don't work, only the taxpayers lose because the politicians and bureaucrats who are responsible for these types of loans and expenditures continue to be re-elected or continue to enjoy their jobs.

Canadair

In 1982, what was the problem at Canadair over the original Challenger aircraft, and how did you become involved?

TERRY GODSELL

Canadair had the burden and the blessing of wide-open government guarantees. The airplane it was trying to sell when I became involved in 1982 was the Challenger 600. It was the heyday of the Saudi Arabian who wanted to go to London to have a good meal. The main specification was the ability to fly between Saudi and London, nonstop, in a particular period of time.

But when the Challenger 600s came off the end of the line and were ready to be delivered, they couldn't meet their performance criteria. The airplane was much heavier in production than it was designed to be and the people who signed contracts originally were guaranteed range and payload.

I was asked by the federal government to go to Canadair in Montreal and see how deep the problem was and whether there was any resolution. When I went in, the Challenger 600 was the only model that had been built. The General Electric–powered Challenger 601, which is the

Challenger of record today, was still a prototype. I discovered that the principal reason a great many of the orders had been placed for the Challenger 600 was that Canadair offered very high rates of interest on the deposit and penalty-free cancellation clauses. The fact that the planes wouldn't perform to the specifications originally promised wasn't very important to the buyers because they could cancel the order right up to the date of delivery and be paid very high interest rates for their deposits.

Most of the buyers never took delivery. Those who did got the airplanes very cheap.

The underlying defect here was the assumption Canadair made that many hundreds of Challenger 600s would be built for a direct cost of X dollars, and sold for X times three. They assumed that once they had sold many hundreds of the planes, they would then be able to absorb all of this direct program cost.

But the program cost was all soft.[3] It was all mush. When we determined that the 600 simply was not going to be an acceptable airplane, the Government of Canada simply wrote off the inventory, or that piece of the inventory that I identified as being soft, for $2.2 billion. And that, I guess, was the first really monstrous federal write-off.

Why was the situation allowed to get as far as it did?

TERRY GODSELL

Because there was nothing in place to stop the process. The bank account was always full because all the loans were guaranteed by the government, and the people involved in the program at the government level, in the Department of Industry, Trade and Commerce, and certainly those people within Canadair, believed that they could work it all out tomorrow.

And the mentality, which was to a significant extent artificially pride-driven, was that we must have a Canadian executive jet.

However, the people at Industry, Trade and Commerce were not qualified to make a judgment. They were professional bureaucrats who were not technically qualified and they depended on the professional opinions of the people at Canadair.

People in government need things to do. And since they need things to do, they find things to do. And some of the things they find to do are very expensive. And one of the things they found to do that was very expensive happened to be in the airplane business!

NOTES

---

1. Loan guarantees are another form of subsidy and they aren't just given by provincial governments. In 1991 the auditor general of Canada estimated that the potential liabilities stemming from federal loan guarantees totalled nearly $8 billion!
2. Magnesium is an element made from magnesite ore. It is used in auto parts, fertilizers, paper, fireworks, etc.
3. Soft costs refer to when the book value is inflated or overly optimistic when compared to the real asset value.

CHAPTER 8

THE MONOPOLY GAME: ONTARIO HYDRO

IAN BAINES
ELIZABETH BRUBAKER
MARCEL CÔTÉ
STEVE PROBYN
LARRY SOLOMON

A s we moved across the country we sardonically christened our trip "The Hunt for the White Elephants." We kept discovering huge structures and hearing about the massive amounts of money that had gone into building them. These costs naturally had all been piled onto the national debt. Whenever we asked what happened to the people who were responsible for the decisions to go ahead with these money-losing projects, all we got for an answer was a shrug.

In Ontario we found the largest white elephant of all. Sitting in the visitors' centre at the Darlington nuclear plant near Toronto, we heard about monopolies and how Ontario Hydro had snagged the largest loan guarantee in Canadian history.

— The Team

What is your definition of a monopoly?

LARRY SOLOMON

A monopoly is an agreement between industry and government that consumers should be robbed of choices. It's an agreement to make decisions in a centralized fashion and eliminate choices for the public at large. Monopolies cannot exist without a conspiracy between governments and industry. Without legislation, without governments, we would find that 99 percent of the monopolies currently in Canada would disappear.

MARCEL CÔTÉ

The problem with Ontario Hydro is that it's a big monopoly. It has always been shielded from the pressure of competition, which would have forced it to change continuously. Because it was not able to change, it ended up in a crisis. Its huge debt has nothing to do with the taxpayer. It has to do with the politicians who decided that Ontario Hydro would be a monopoly.

STEVE PROBYN

If you go down University Avenue in Toronto, you walk past the Hydro building and then farther down you'll see a statue of Sir Adam Beck, who invented public power in this country. In the early part of the 20th century Beck wanted to introduce public power to every farm and hamlet in Ontario. He wanted it available to the working man. But as things progressed, the idealism behind the drive to public power became entrenched in a bureaucracy and it became ossified in bureaucratic form.

LARRY SOLOMON

Adam Beck was a visionary and a politician who saw an opportunity to create an empire for himself. He wanted his empire to be completely unaccountable. He was very clear about this. He felt that he should be free from any provincial control. Of course, it's a good thing not to have political interference because politicians can do a lot of damage.

The idea was to bring cheap power from Niagara to the municipalities in Ontario. Ontario Hydro was going to be strictly a vehicle for carrying that power through the transmission lines. But instead of being the friendly co-op, servicing the various municipalities and bringing in power that was generated by private sources, Ontario Hydro decided to take over those sources. Then it started taking over the municipal utilities. Over time it just grew and grew and the monopoly made sure that nobody else could generate power in Ontario.

Initially the company tried to dam every river in the province. And then it decided that mega coal plants should be built everywhere. Then it decided that mega nuclear plants should be built everywhere. In fact, it made a lot of very expensive, very serious and poor choices about the technologies that would be viable. Today coal and nuclear technologies, which are the basis of the Ontario Hydro system, are outdated technologies. And what is viable is being shut out of the province.

The problem was that there were no checks and balances. There weren't any shareholders. And customers had no choices. There were no competitors. It was the Adam Beck empire. Something that started off being a benign democracy in the end became very pernicious.

ELIZABETH BRUBAKER

Because it was a monopoly, Ontario Hydro was able to get away with behaviour that under other circumstances wouldn't have been possible. Ontario Hydro has done a tremendous amount of damage to Aboriginal communities by damming rivers and flooding lands. It's destroyed fisheries; it's eroded riverbanks and lakeshores. It's destroyed the way of life of many Aboriginal communities that depend on the rivers. Many of them are still suffering from the dams that were built decades ago.

For example, during the 1940s the company wanted more power to be generated at Niagara Falls. In order to do that it needed to put more water through its turbines. It decided to divert the Ogoki River in northern Ontario, a river that would normally flow north into the Albany River and ultimately into James Bay. Hydro built some dams and channels and diverted the river southward so that it flowed down the Little Jackfish River into Lake Nipigon, down the Nipigon River and into Lake Superior. And then from Lake Superior it flowed through Lake Huron and Lake Erie and finally through Ontario Hydro's turbines. And wreaked havoc on the environment.

Ontario Hydro flooded 89 square miles, causing an enormous amount of erosion. The flooding contaminated the fish with mercury, and the Native people living in the area suffered terribly. Fisheries were destroyed and traditional hunting grounds were flooded. People are still paying a terrible price for this diversion.

LARRY SOLOMON

As Hydro grew, its bureaucracy also grew, and because it's hard to control many small plants with a large bureaucratic structure, as its bureaucracy grew, it needed to build larger and larger plants. The problem was that

Hydro had inherited a lot of small plants from the municipalities when it took them over.

So Hydro went on a program of dismantling, and in some cases dynamiting, some 500 small hydro dams across the province simply because they couldn't be managed from head office in Toronto — and because Hydro didn't want to have a decentralized structure that would allow all of these perfectly fine facilities to be managed in other little municipalities.

IAN BAINES

Some municipalities were exempted from this policy. There are, I believe, 13 Ontario municipalities that generate their own electricity from hydro dams or wood-burning plants. Ontario Hydro is not encouraging this practice and they are raising the rates for these specific utilities. One such utility is in Cornwall. Cornwall Electric has built its own downtown power-generating plant. It's a cogeneration plant and Cornwall District Heating is using it to heat the downtown core, as well as to provide power for downtown Cornwall. The city can get away with generating its own power because it is not a part of Ontario Hydro. It can retain its independent status because it is in a unique corner of Ontario, within an hour of Montreal, and just across the river from New York State. In Cornwall they have generated power since 1910, and they continue to retain independence to buy power — and cheaper power — from Quebec and New York. Since there was no need to connect to Ontario Hydro, they're not bound by the same regulations that Hydro imposes upon other municipalities.

How does Hydro get away with imposing these regulations?

IAN BAINES

Because it's a monopoly. Since 1906 Ontario Hydro has had the ability to provide power at cost in Ontario without any sort of competition. The same sort of system has existed in telephone companies, gas utilities and cable TV for a long time.

Now, to be fair, in the past Hydro did a pretty good job of providing reliable, low-cost power. However, in the 1980s it built some very expensive nuclear power plants, plants that didn't quite live up to their requirements. Consequently the price of power rose by almost 100 percent over the past 12 years. When you have a monopoly, you have the ability to regulate your own market, and you can get away with things like a 100 percent price rise over a dozen years. If you had a truly competitive market, you'd have had other companies coming in and providing power at their own cost.[1]

LARRY SOLOMON

Initially Ontario Hydro was skeptical about nuclear technology, but the federal bureaucrats felt that nuclear power was the fuel of the future.

So Hydro agreed to build the first Pickering nuclear plant. And then over time Ontario Hydro developed its own nuclear elite, who of course thought that nuclear generating stations would be the answer to all of their problems. At that point Hydro's program was pretty well exclusively one of building nuclear plants.

Now, when Ontario Hydro goes to the politicians at Queen's Park and tells them we must have this plant or the lights are going to go out in this province, the politicians are not in a position to assess whether that's true or not. They have no one else to turn to. There are no competing providers of power who can offer a sober second thought. They are captive to Ontario Hydro claims. The simplest thing for them to do is to throw up their hands and say, "I guess that's what we must do."

The Hydro bureaucracy is able to dictate the policies of the Ministry of Energy instead of the other way around. When the Darlington nuclear power plant was being debated in the mid-1970s, I was in the gallery watching the process and wondering how such an important decision could take place on the basis of no information. The politicians were not interested in the debate. For most of it three-quarters of them didn't even bother to be in the room. When it was time to vote they all came in and voted against having any scrutiny of whether the Darlington plant would be needed. They said that the plant was so urgent that we couldn't afford to have any public analysis to prove it. They were interested only in coming into the chamber after the debate was over and rubber-stamping the decision that Ontario Hydro had made for society. They had no spine to challenge Ontario Hydro.

What I saw was an apathetic legislature, a powerless legislature that couldn't get a grip on the issues that were put before them. They had billion-dollar decisions to make about a technology over which there was great public concern. Yet they had no way of scrutinizing the project that was going to proceed. They had no way of standing up to a

Crown corporation that they were presumably there to control. The Crown corporation was not accountable to the legislature because it was not accountable to anyone. But the legislators weren't accountable to the public either. Legislators were there just going through the motions.

STEVE PROBYN

The problem with the Darlington station is not that it doesn't work, not that it produces electricity inefficiently, it's that it cost $15 billion to build. As a result there's this enormous stranded debt, which as markets progress and as electricity prices are reduced in response to competitive pressures, somebody will have to deal with. Is it the people who lent the money? Is it the ratepayers or is it the shareholders, i.e., the taxpayers? Does Hydro go bankrupt?

One of the great debates will be how to deal with this debt. The people who own the debt are the taxpayers and ratepayers of Ontario, who are, respectively, the owners and customers of Ontario Hydro.

How did Hydro get the money to build the Darlington complex?

LARRY SOLOMON

Ontario Hydro borrowed with government guarantees. The immense debt of $35 billion is backed up by assets, many of which have very little value.[2]

If Ontario Hydro had to borrow on its own nickel, if it had to go to the bond market and tell bondholders that it would be paying back those bonds without any government assurance, Hydro would find that it couldn't borrow any money at all. Hydro doesn't have any credit rating. It's the Ontario government that has a credit rating. We, the taxpayers, lend the money to the Ontario government and they turn around and lend it to Ontario Hydro.

So Hydro has been speculating with public money?

LARRY SOLOMON

Hydro certainly has been speculating with taxpayers' money. There's no downside for Hydro if its projects go belly-up. There's an upside if one of these projects happens to work, but most of the time they don't work. Most of the time they're boondoggles and the taxpayer ends up holding the bag.

The nuclear industry is the largest boondoggle in Canadian corporate history because plants have been built that are worth less than the construction cost. There isn't anybody in the business world who would pay a dime for nuclear plants if they also had to assume the liabilities that went along with them. Nuclear power is not economic. Nobody is building nuclear plants except Third World countries, who either have them given to them or who want them for bomb-making purposes. Canada has only been able to sell plants to people who will take them for free or who will accept bribes.

Ontario Hydro was the last company to abandon nuclear power in the Western world. The last reactors to be completed were ordered in 1976. It took until the 1990s for those plants to be finished.

But Ontario Hydro has learned from its mistakes. It's not planning to build any more nuclear plants. The problem is that it learned its mistake after accumulating a $35-billion debt. The Darlington complex, which opened in 1990 and which was initially estimated to cost between $3 billion and $3.5 billion, ultimately cost $15 billion. Hydro built Darlington, and cost overruns were something in the order of $12 billion. But nobody lost his job, nobody was demoted.

How efficient is Ontario Hydro's use of fuel?

IAN BAINES

Ontario Hydro operates at about 33 percent efficiency. In other words, one-third of the uranium or coal or oil that's used to make the electricity actually turns into electricity. The other two-thirds is wasted. It's eventually dumped into the lake. I'm sure the fish in Lake Ontario appreciate it but it doesn't do any economic good.

By using cogeneration, which uses natural gas instead, your efficiency would go from 33 percent to 90 percent just like that. Natural gas produces the least amount of greenhouse gas and carbon dioxide of any of the fossil fuels. It doesn't make smoke, it doesn't make soot, it doesn't make sulphur dioxide. Private power producers have to meet the 1994 environmental requirements. Ontario Hydro doesn't meet any of them.

None of the Hydro power-generating plants meets any of the current regulations. When Hydro built their coal plants, there were only minimum, if any, environmental regulations. And now every year the regulations get tougher and tougher. The only reason Hydro doesn't have to meet them is that it built the plants 20 or 30 years ago and there's no money in the pot for Hydro to go out and retrofit these plants. Ontario Hydro is one of the largest polluters in the province because these plants produce very large volumes of sulphurous and nitrous oxides.

LARRY SOLOMON

If legislation like the Environmental Assessment Act (1976) comes along and gets in Hydro's way, Hydro lobbies for exemptions, and because it's so close to government, it gets those exemptions.

ELIZABETH BRUBAKER

If there's an accident at Darlington and your property is damaged, you can't sue Hydro. An accident at Darlington is covered by a law called the Nuclear Liability Act, which was passed by the federal government in 1976 and proclaimed in 1980. If there's an accident with costs over $75 million dollars, Ontario Hydro is not responsible. The act was passed because no insurance company could take on the responsibility for a nuclear accident, which is a pretty good sign that nuclear accidents might result in the kind of costs that are simply unacceptable to society.

LARRY SOLOMON

This act also states that if there is an accident at a nuclear plant in Canada, and if that accident is caused by a faulty part supplied by General Electric or Westinghouse or anyone else, no matter how much damage that accident causes (and it could wipe out the City of Toronto), GE shareholders wouldn't have to put up a nickel in compensation. GE has to stand behind its toaster ovens, but it doesn't have to stand behind its nuclear parts. These companies realized that nuclear technology was far too dangerous for them to stand behind their products. So they said to Hydro, "Look, if we have to be liable for the parts we produce for you, we'll refuse to supply you." And Hydro said, "Don't worry. We can take care of that problem." They went to the federal government and this law was the result.

The Nuclear Liability Act was not a contentious issue when it was passed. Nuclear technology was not questioned by anyone. There really were very few people to question the technology, apart from some citizens' groups.

Industry saw a cash cow. It had guaranteed profits. And there was no one there to question the wisdom of removing liability for the most dangerous technology that has ever been developed.

Is that why private companies haven't invested in the nuclear industry?

LARRY SOLOMON

Private companies have invested in the nuclear industry, but only when they've had government guarantees. The technology is too risky for the private sector to accept.

When Margaret Thatcher decided to privatize the U.K.'s entire electricity industry, there was the widespread view that nuclear power was the way of the future. Business believed it, government believed it and a good part of the public believed it. But when the assets were finally put on the market, prospective purchasers, after they had a chance to look at the books, realized that they could not afford to buy the nuclear assets. They were keen to buy the fossil fuel assets and the hydraulic assets. They were keen to buy the distribution companies, but they balked at buying the nuclear plants. They felt that the risk was just too high.

The result was that the rest of the system was privatized. There is now a competitive system in Britain, but those nuclear plants could not be sold. They're now in a Crown corporation called Nuclear Electric. And that company is going to be running those plants until they die.

STEVE PROBYN

In Britain it took political will to move forward with the restructuring and disaggregation of the various components of the electrical supply industry. Political will is the missing ingredient here. The other ingredients are technology — that's here — and capital, which is here in abundance. The privatization of Nova Scotia Power has shown that we can restructure the electricity industry in Canada. All that's missing here in Ontario is political will.

How has this monopoly affected Ontario's economy?

IAN BAINES

You and I are paying very high electric power rates. And the jobs that we have are directly proportionate to the amount of investment in Ontario. Any large company considering expanding into Ontario now has to face

74

the fact that power here is among the most expensive in Canada. The economy suffers because car factories don't locate here, steel companies won't build here, so no new jobs are created. A lot of Ontario's infra-structure has to stay here. It can't move. But any business that's mobile will jump ship.

LARRY SOLOMON

Industries left because they couldn't tolerate the environment that had developed. Nobody can bail out of the Hydro system except by leaving the province. The entire economy is distorted by the megaprojects and the power of monopolies and their collaboration with governments. The credit rating of the province has been downgraded in large part because of megaprojects such as Darlington. Megaprojects are endeav-ours that only governments can love.

What's the future for Ontario Hydro?

LARRY SOLOMON

Ontario Hydro needs to be broken up. Various components of it have to be sold off. The ones that can't be sold off, such as the nuclear plants, should be put into a separate Crown corporation. Those plants can be run until they're no longer safe and then shut down permanently.

IAN BAINES

But don't forget that Hydro has left no provision for decommissioning these plants. Where do you put the spent fuel? What do you do with the building after it's been shut down but still remains radioactive for many years? Those are hidden costs that Hydro hasn't taken into account and will have to deal with someday.

I think Ontario Hydro is going to collapse under the weight of its own debt and be bailed out by the government. When that happens we'll have a fiasco that Ontario doesn't need.[3]

NOTES

1. The Energy Competition Act was passed by the Ontario govern-ment in October 1998 to allow for competition in the marketplace,

and it went into effect in 2000. Ontario Hydro was divided into five successor companies in 1999.

2. 1995 figures. In 2002 Ontario Hydro's liabilities amounted to $38.1 billion. This figure includes the cost of decommissioning nuclear power stations and disposing of atomic waste. Ontario Hydro's successor companies share responsibility for $17.2 billion of this total, and $13.1 billion will be covered by "dedicated revenue streams," i.e., energy taxes. The remaining $7.8 billion is considered stranded debt and is being managed by one of the successor companies: the Ontario Electricity Financial Corporation (OEFC).

3. On April 1, 1999, Ontario Hydro was divided into five successor companies. On May 1, 2002, the industry was deregulated. Two of the five successor companies (Ontario Power Generation Inc. and Hydro One) are private companies, another two (the Independent Electricity Market Operator and the Electrical Safety Authority) are not-for-profit organizations, and one (Ontario Electricity Financial Corporation) is a Crown Corporation.

---— PART THREE ——————

THE SUBSIDY SYNDROME

CHAPTER 9

EXPANDING THE OIL PATCH

WILF GOBERT
RALPH HEDLIN
GERARD PROTTI

A *t an oil derrick in Carstairs, Alberta, north of Calgary, we talked with some industry analysts about the National Energy Program, one of the most controversial government subsidies ever instituted in Western Canada. The program, which was in effect from 1980 to 1984 after a series of world oil price jumps, was an attempt by the federal government to call the shots as to where wells would be drilled and by whom. This behaviour resulted in a glaring increase, still evident today, of suspicion and bad will between Western Canadians and Ottawa.*

— The Team

GERARD PROTTI

Back in 1974 when the first Arab oil embargo occurred, world oil prices jumped and it looked as if they were going to continue to rise at fairly high rates over the next few years.

WILF GOBERT

The Western world, North America in particular, was worried about the security of the oil supply. We had been cut off by the Arabs, and there was concern we were running out of secure oil and gas produced indigenously.

GERARD PROTTI

The Canadian government made the same decision that a number of other governments around the world made to protect consumers: they would keep prices low and slowly start the rise to world levels. In Canada, because we are blessed with bountiful resources of oil and gas, the feeling was that we could keep our competitive advantage longer by keeping those prices low. That decision resulted in distortions coming into the economy. It introduced an era of heavy government intervention in the industry that culminated in 1980 in the National Energy Program, which had a negative impact on the economy and the oil industry.

WILF GOBERT

Consumers were being subsidized in terms of the price they were paying for energy. It has been estimated that about $55 billion was paid by the government from 1974 to 1985, the period during which prices were controlled below world level. So consumers were being subsidized and encouraged into wasteful consumption.

GERARD PROTTI

If you are paying 20 or 30 or 40 percent less than people in other countries for your gasoline, and you think gas is going to remain cheap for the foreseeable future, when you go out to buy your next car, this is going to influence your decision — whether you buy a Volkswagen, or the big Buick, loaded. Consumers were not getting the right signals about the true cost of gasoline on the world market.

RALPH HEDLIN

By lowering the cost, the government encouraged people to use more energy. But when the prices came up, industrial areas were not adapted to high oil prices, whereas their competitors south of the border were. So by transferring this money to the Ontario consumers the government damaged the industrial heartland of Ontario.

WILF GOBERT

The government was also using taxation revenues to provide grants to the oil industry to invest in a way that it thought would be more profitable for future generations. Government policy was to encourage Canadian ownership and as a result we had a national oil company, Petro-Canada, that was an arm of government policy and was using public money to buy companies away from the private sector at extravagant prices.

EXPANDING THE OIL PATCH

Whose brainy idea was that?

RALPH HEDLIN

Oh, it was to be a window on the industry. It was to allow bureaucrats in Ottawa to have somebody they could phone up and find out all about the oil industry. It was just a silly, specious thing and there was no real justification of any kind.

WILF GOBERT

The total value of Petro-Canada was about $10 billion, but when energy prices fell in the late 1980s that $10 billion was worth possibly $3 billion.[1]

We should, however, distinguish the Petro-Canada of the 1970s and the first half of the 1980s, which was an arm of government policy, from today's Petro-Canada, which is owned to a significant extent by shareholders and is operating to generate a profit. Today it's a healthy company.

How did the government implement the decision to subsidize the oil industry?

GERARD PROTTI

The government wanted to encourage the development of a very broad energy base within Canada. Their solution was to subsidize, through grants, the drilling of oil and natural gas prospects and exploration in the Beaufort Sea, the Arctic Islands, offshore Labrador and the Atlantic Coast offshore. But they knew that these were high-cost resources compared to the resources in Western Canada and the Western sedimentary basin, and because so much of the cost would be offset through grants, they drove companies to get involved.

WILF GOBERT

In order to force industry to invest in areas it felt were uneconomic, the government taxed the revenue of energy production and then gave it back to those who were willing to spend in the prescribed manner. So we have the absurd example of taxing production in Western Canada, where people were making money, and then using those revenues to drill holes in the Arctic Ocean — and these wells were costing $50 million or $100 million each. For that amount of money you could drill 200 wells in Western Canada.

In the Beaufort Sea, for instance, you can drill for only three months of the year because it's ice-infested the rest of the time. Over the course of this period of subsidy the oil industry spent well in excess of $1 billion, possibly as high as $2 billion, drilling something like 15 or 20 wells. The companies found hydrocarbons, they found oil and they found natural gas. It's what geologists would call a technical success. We proved that it's there. However, the economic value wouldn't be a whole lot different if they had paid all of us very handsomely to dig a hole in the ground that nobody was going to use.

So we have a massive piece of infrastructure up in the Arctic pumping out no gas!

WILF GOBERT

There's no activity taking place up there now. We have some glorious hundred-million-dollar holes that have no value because the science is such that you have to permanently plug them in a manner that no oil or gas will ever leak out of them. So they're never going to be usable.

RALPH HEDLIN

What we witnessed was a raid on the resources of the oil industry in order to enhance the position of consumers in the major consuming provinces by holding the prices down. It was an enormous transfer that distorted economic development. Had in fact that money been shared in some sensible way, Alberta would have grown more rapidly. These decisions tremendously lessened the efficiency of capital use.

WILF GOBERT

The rate of drilling success in Western Canada averages about 70 percent for both oil and natural gas. When you find oil the wealth of the country goes up for everybody: the investor makes money from having drilled the hole, the provincial government takes a royalty, the oil company makes a profit and the government takes income tax. If the money had been invested in Western Canada instead of the 50 or so wells in the Arctic, we could have drilled 8,000 wells. At today's oil prices each well would generate a revenue of about $4 million. With a 100 percent success rate, you would have had $32 billion. Since royalties average 20 percent, the Alberta government would have made $6.5 billion. That's $6.5 billion of government money that wouldn't have had to come from taxing the people. The government didn't get it because the money was spent on holes that will never produce oil and gas.

GERARD PROTTI

A lot of the justification for this intrusion, you have to remember, was the belief that the price of oil was going to be $100 a barrel and higher. Natural gas, they thought, was going to be several times higher than what it is today. The belief was that we were going to run out of this resource, and that the technology couldn't be developed to keep bringing in new supplies on a competitive basis. All those assumptions, whether made by politicians or people in industry or consumers, failed.

What people realize now is that in a free market you've got all the conditions present to move forward and generate technologies and survive quite nicely in a volatile commodity market. Most countries that didn't have their own source of energy went automatically to world levels because they had no other choice. They had to invest immediately in new technologies and develop new approaches that allowed them to use less energy in their economy and encourage the development of energy-efficient technology and energy-saving consumption. But in Canada, because of government decisions, we postponed the point at which we brought new technologies into the economy and we spent a lot of dollars that would have been more fruitfully spent in the Western sedimentary basin, where we know the resource is present in vast quantities.

RALPH HEDLIN

I think you can say, in a nutshell, that the government moved in and replaced the market. They taxed the gross revenues of many of the smaller companies. They encouraged companies like Dome and many others to go into the Arctic with subsidies, the taxpayers' money, and it's all disappeared. It's sunk in the Beaufort Sea, in the Melville Peninsula, in the Labrador Straits, on the Scotian Shelf, and it's all gone. We get nothing, and our children get nothing, from it. It's all gone.

They took the business decisions out of an area where the marketplace really dictated where people should be and distorted the market by pouring in taxpayers' revenues. These were decisions taken by politicians and bureaucrats in Ottawa who didn't know a pint of oil from a pint of milk.

WILF GOBERT

One of the realities in Canada is that when it comes to energy, and to some extent food production, the large population centres with the consumers and the majority of the electorate are in one section of the country and the energy production is in another. There are no votes to determine whether the oil industry agrees; it's all decided by what the central government thinks is best.

RALPH HEDLIN

Had those energy resources been in the province of Ontario, with the government caucus being what it was — a lot of MPs from Ontario, none from the West — not one policy of this kind would have been initiated. The market, not the government, would have driven the industry.

WILF GOBERT

We're kind of blaming governments here, but the oil industry was not totally pure and clean in this process. One of the problems with subsidy is that it causes private sector companies to do things they might not otherwise do. But they do them thinking they are going to get an advantage. A subsidy is the transfer of an advantage. Somebody pays for it and somebody is going to take advantage of it.

What happened in the oil industry was that Canadian-owned companies had an advantage over foreign-controlled companies. So at the beginning of the National Energy Program in the early 1980s, some of Canada's best Canadian-owned companies, like Dome Petroleum, borrowed money to buy assets in Canada away from foreigners. The foreigners ended up selling at very high prices and the Canadian companies had to borrow huge amounts of money to pay them.

Then interest rates went through the roof in the early 1980s. Energy prices subsequently declined and our Canadian companies went bankrupt. The foreigners had taken their money out of the country and invested elsewhere. Canadian companies, along with the shareholders' money, investors' money, went down the tube. At its peak Dome Petroleum was worth several billion dollars, trading at $25 a share — and it went to virtually zero.

GERARD PROTTI

When financial markets see government influencing the marketplace, they start demonstrating a lot of concern. During that period financial markets were actually shying away from the industry because they saw that it was highly regulated by a highly interventionist government. So we had a double-whammy: the drying up of equity markets and of interest in the industry.

What happened to the National Energy Program?

GERARD PROTTI

Canadians realized that it had caused enough problems and we began the process of deregulation. Shortly after we deregulated, world oil prices fell and some tough times followed.

WILF GOBERT

But once we went into deregulation, free market prices and the profitable use of capital attracted investors in the development of new oil companies, to the extent that today the level of Canadian investment is higher than it was at the peak of the government program. New companies controlled by Canadians are investing their money profitably in finding oil and gas that is economic.

GERARD PROTTI

The result is an industry that is leaner, more efficient and able to compete on a global basis. It's showing signs of increased activity, employment and economic growth.

What lesson can we learn from the failure of the NEP?

WILF GOBERT

It's a lesson you can use in any industry. Governments are not in power to compete with the private sector. We can't have an arm of government policy competing with a company that's trying to make money for its investors. You can't have them operating side by side. If a free enterprise company is not willing to put its money into a program, then the taxpayers should not want to have their money put into it either.

RALPH HEDLIN

When people in government move into the private sector, they are not doing a good job running the government. Their objectives are totally different from those of the marketplace because they're responsive not to shareholders, but to electors. Government should stay out of business, other than to regulate it to ensure there aren't abuses and that the environment is protected. Government has no business whatsoever getting into the combining of land, labour and capital with the objective of making wealth.

NOTES

1. The drop in value was not only a result of falling oil prices. Petro-Canada began selling off its assets in preparation for privatization.

--------- CHAPTER 10 ---------

THE FARMER AT THE WELL

JOHN DUVENAUD

CLAY GILSON

ALLAN JOHNSTON

KEITH LEWIS

JIM PALLISTER

BARRY PRENTICE

RICHARD WRIGHT

*T*here's an image, ingrained in many of our minds, of the lonely Prairie farmer, plow and team of faithful horses standing against the sky (which really does seem bigger in the West), toiling in the field from sunup till deep into the night, relying on his brain and muscles to tame the whims of nature. Usually this image is in black and white because we've all seen The Grapes of Wrath.

In contrast, the turn-of-the-century reality is in living colour, and includes cellphones, computers, satellites and other state-of-the-art technology, as farmers market many of their products to customers half a world away. They are, however, still at the mercy of the whims of nature, among other things.

As we discovered, the agricultural community, which has been the largest recipient of government funds in Canada, is split between those who are anxious to maintain the status quo and those, mostly young farmers, who want to escape the government's domination, and trust in their own ability to control their lives. But seven years after our first trip West there are increas-

ingly boisterous demands from many in the farm community for Ottawa's help.

— The Team

How did farmers get so hooked on subsidies?

CLAY GILSON

For a long time Canada didn't subsidize farmers the way the United States did. It was only in the 1960s that we started to get into the subsidy game. And even when we got involved we resisted the formula approach. It was more ad hoc for emergencies, drought and so on. As time went on the farmers pressed more and more for formula pricing and price supports. The biggest and most dramatic pressure came in the 1980s. The Common Market in Europe had developed some strength and started to challenge the United States and world markets. And the U.S. and Europe met head-on in terms of subsidy. On both sides enormous sums of money were poured into export subsidies, hurting countries such as Australia and Canada.

By 1986 there was absolute chaos, and Canadian farmers began to say they had been badly side swiped by this subsidy war and therefore wanted government to help, and the government did move in with fairly major subsidies. As a result, government support and government regulatory activity has been very extensive in the industry. I would say that from 1986 through to 1990, government payments into the grain industry in Saskatchewan were equivalent to the farmers' net income. Without government payments there would have been no net farm income in that province.

KEITH LEWIS

I believe that production subsidies, those based on producing grain, have distorted farmers' planting decisions over the years. Farmers didn't respond to market signals. They responded to what they thought were going to be the best returns based on government programs. Subsidies encouraged the planting of grain on land that might have been used for other purposes. Some programs encouraged them to bring more marginal land into production. As a result, land was brought into production that was highly erodible, causing environmental consequences. The land either washed away or it blew away.

But farmers are really quite adept at making the best use of government programs, and you could probably tick your calendar off every fall after harvest, when the farmers made their annual migration to Ottawa to look for more government support.

Were you part of this yearly migration to Ottawa?

KEITH LEWIS

Yes. Back in the late 1980s I was involved with the Saskatchewan Canola Growers Association. We were part of the larger agricultural infrastructure in the province, involved in lobbying Ottawa for subsidies for Western farmers. We were successful, too. The federal and provincial governments all came through with very large amounts of money for Western farmers.

What was the intended purpose of the subsidies?

KEITH LEWIS

The government's stated purpose was to address what was viewed as a short-term problem in agriculture. But what they failed to realize was that this problem had been going on for some time, was going to continue and in fact would get worse over the years. And of course that only resulted in demands for more money. On one occasion in particular the prime minister, the minister of agriculture and deputy ministers, and probably 30 of us from Western Canada, met in a room in the Centre Block in Ottawa; as a result of that lobbying effort Brian Mulroney and his government pumped over $1 billion into the economy of Western Canada.

But I was never really convinced that this was the best way of solving the ills of agriculture, and neither was the organization I worked with. However, in the politics of farm organizations in Saskatchewan, it was important to appear to be unified, to have a clear voice coming from Western Canada. We were very much under the influence of subsidies in other countries. What was happening in Western Canada was the result of what other governments were doing in Europe and the United States.

CLAY GILSON

Now, farmers will be quick to tell you — and I think it's to some degree true — that they didn't derive the full benefit of those subsidies. The money didn't all go to them directly. It was passed on in the form of money to transportation and servicing of input industries. The subsidies have been a benefit to the whole system, not just the farmers.

KEITH LEWIS

The people who benefited from production-based subsidies were not the farmers. The ones who benefited were the banks that needed the money, the grain companies that needed the grain, the railroads that needed the grain to haul to port, and the list goes on.

When was the subsidy to transport grain introduced?

BARRY PRENTICE

The subsidy to transport grain originated because of a deal in 1897 between one of the railways and the government to put a line into southern British Columbia, to maintain the sovereignty of the country in competition with the potential U.S. railways coming in. There was a subsidy, generally referred to as the Crow Rate, for settlers' effects coming out to the West, and for transporting grain to the coast.[1] This low rate was established in perpetuity from all of the sites that this railway had at the time. However, as the Prairies were developed, there were more railways and more elevators, and suddenly there was an inequity between those who ran the original elevators and those who ran the new ones.

As a result, in the 1920s the government made the Crow Rate a statutory rate for all elevators and all railways to all points. This was fine for quite a while because productivity increased and there wasn't much inflation. But in the late 1950s costs were no longer sustained by the revenues of this fixed rate and the railways started to lose money.

The major inefficiency in the grain business, for which the Crow Rate was responsible, was backtracking. The railways got paid the Crow Rate only if the grain was taken from the Prairies out to one of the ports: Thunder Bay or Vancouver.

ALLAN JOHNSTON

If I wanted to ship oats out of Saskatchewan to Minneapolis, I couldn't ship it to Winnipeg and then down the railroad to Minneapolis. Couldn't do that. Instead it went to Thunder Bay to get the subsidy rate, and then it was hauled back to Winnipeg and then it could go to Minneapolis! This process tied up that railcar probably two or three weeks longer than it should have. And there was all that expense of hauling the car to Thunder Bay and back to Winnipeg because somebody wouldn't sign a piece of paper that said, "Turn that thing south at Winnipeg!"

JIM PALLISTER

The freight subsidy really hurt development here because it forced the export of raw grain out of Western Canada. Now, in a country where the stated objective is to encourage industry, to add value to raw products rather than exporting raw products, why would you have a subsidy of the export of raw grain? It's hurt the livestock industry in Western Canada and it's been a disincentive toward milling and food processing in Western Canada. It's basically been a disincentive toward living in Western Canada.

JOHN DUVENAUD

It was the most poisonous program that we've ever had in Western Canada. It was a program where we borrowed $700 million a year and gave it to the railroads. That money was used to pay foreigners to take our best raw product out of the country and process it somewhere else.

Did it cost jobs?

KEITH LEWIS

Of course it did. With the Crow Rate in place, why would you divert grain to a flour mill or a pasta plant? We don't have any of those things in Western Canada, but there are four pasta production plants in North Dakota, all operating on durum wheat from Canada or North Dakota, and the jobs are all in North Dakota. There isn't one single job produced here in Saskatchewan, even though they're using our grain.

RICHARD WRIGHT

This subsidy was probably the most idiotic practice of economic mis-management you could ever devise for a region like ours. It stifled the development of industry here. For many years all of the jobs from value-added processing have appeared in regions outside of Saskatchewan, even as close as Alberta. When you ask Albertans where they came from, chances are that one out of two will say that they came from Saskatchewan.

ALLAN JOHNSTON

Young people are leaving by the thousands every year. We educate them and then they're just gone. They're going to Alberta to work in the oil industry. They're going to B.C., to Toronto or to the U.S. They're going abroad. They're just leaving.

RICHARD WRIGHT

The population of Saskatchewan grew very quickly in the early part of the century, up to one million people in the 1920s. Since then some seven or eight million people have been born here but the population's still about a million. Where have they all gone? They've gone somewhere else to get a job because there are no jobs here.

Do you think there will ever be a time when subsidies to agriculture are no longer necessary?

CLAY GILSON

In the short run I don't think that we can do without some subsidies because the whole infrastructure is based on past policies. But the current attitude in the rural communities is to look for less and less government support. When you go to these communities now, you see amazing changes. They're doing things they wouldn't have thought of doing 10 years ago. They know they have to find ways to become more self-sufficient.

KEITH LEWIS

I would like to see subsidies out of agriculture completely. We've created a tremendous burden on the taxpayers in this country with all of these various programs and institutions, and it's cost enormous amounts of money to sustain them. The people of Canada can't afford them.

NOTES

1. The Crow Rate was called the Western Grain Transportation Act after 1983, when the subsidy was no longer paid to the producers of the grain, the farmers, but directly to the railway which moved the grain. This subsidy was eliminated in 1995.

CHAPTER 11

ALL "A BOARD"

TED ALLEN
JOHN DUVENAUD
CLAY GILSON
JIM HARRIMAN
JOHN HODGE

ALLAN JOHNSTON
GRAHAM KEDGLEY
KEITH LEWIS
JIM PALLISTER
FRED RANDLE

*P*robably the most ubiquitous institution in Western Canada is the Canadian Wheat Board. It seemed to be everywhere and played a part in every discussion we had in the West. All of the farmers we talked to brought the CWB into the conversation. Somebody even likened it to an octopus with tentacles reaching into every province of the country, although its hold is most tenacious in the West. A powerful and controversial organization, it dominates the agricultural world and is the topic of hours of spirited and sometimes angry conversation from Winkler to Wellwyn.
— The Team

KEITH LEWIS

The Wheat Board has become irrelevant in today's world.

ALLAN JOHNSTON

The Canadian Wheat Board was set up in 1935 to market grain and to protect farmers. No technology was available then and there weren't many roads. Most farmers didn't have trucks and they were getting ripped off by some grain companies because the grain companies were in control of the whole situation.

CLAY GILSON

At first farmers had a choice: they could market through the Wheat Board or they could use the open market. But during the war regulations were put into place and the board handled all of the marketing. After the war a plebiscite was held to decide whether there'd be open or Wheat Board marketing and the farmers agreed they wanted the board to be the central selling agency. The Wheat Board is the sales agent for wheat and barley. There are other crops that are not on the board, and these are sold on the open market.

JIM PALLISTER

The stated purpose of the Canadian Wheat Board is to maximize the returns of wheat and barley to Western Canadian farmers. The main problem with the board is that it's a monopoly. As a monopoly it is unable to adequately service the changing and dynamic world markets that we have now. Farmers have got the technology that they didn't have when the Wheat Board was set up in the horse-and-buggy days. Back then they needed that marketing agent to help them merchandise their products. Now farmers should be released from the monopoly's control and the Wheat Board should be made voluntary again.

JOHN DUVENAUD

The way it's structured now, the board reports to the federal minister of agriculture. It could just as easily operate under a board of directors of farmers. Then it would certainly have a far clearer mandate.

JIM PALLISTER

There's a movement in Western Canada to free the market and liberate us from this high-cost, inefficient system that doesn't have to compete. If we were free to sell our products ourselves and go around that system, we would then have the leverage to make the other players more efficient.

We're not talking about taking anything apart. We're talking about building a team approach between the people who want to do their own business and find their own markets and those who want the Wheat Board there as a stabilizing influence and another marketing option. It would lead to a more co-operative approach.

Right now the Wheat Board system is not co-operative, it's coercive. We're required to deliver our grain to the board. Some farmers believe that the Wheat Board should continue to be a monopoly. They believe that somehow the government can look after us better than we can ourselves. The Wheat Board has built up trust with people. It stabilizes prices and reduces risk.

The Wheat Board handles all our money. The money from all of the wheat that leaves Western Canada goes into the Wheat Board and is eventually distributed to us. But that happens only after everybody else takes their cut: the railroads, the various unions, the port facilities along the line and the Wheat Board itself. We get what's left.

With an open market we'd be able to make a deal in advance for the total price of our grain, so we'd know what we were going to get before we even delivered that grain. In the case of the Wheat Board crops, I don't know for a year and a half what I'm going to get for this year's crop! I call it "Lotto Wheat Board."

FRED RANDLE

Nobody else in the world operates a business like we do. We don't know for 18 months what we're going to get for our product. We set up this year, we grow the grain next year, then 18 months later we find out what we're going to get.

The newer generation of farmers needs cash flow. They have commitments. The Wheat Board can put farmers in a severe financial situation if they gear up for certain operations and then all of a sudden the board doesn't want their grain.

Once the Wheat Board said we had too much wheat and we needed a LIFT program, which meant Lower Inventories for Tomorrow. They paid us to seed our land down to grass. It distorted everything so badly that pretty soon we had all this grass, but we didn't have any wheat to sell!

JOHN DUVENAUD

The Wheat Board has done a lot of good for a lot of farmers over a long period of time. But we've come to a turning point, and farmers now know that we can market export grain on our own.

We just didn't grow up with the idea of marketing. Most Prairie farmers were out doing summer fallow when they were 11 years old, and setting the combine when they were 18, but they've been protected from having to do their own marketing. But now more than

95

half the grain is sold on the open market — canola, flax, rye, oats, peas, lentils — and farmers have figured out how to handle that market quite effectively.

Having learned that you can market your own lentils, canola and flax, the idea that you can market your own wheat, too, is not that strange. Now farmers know that they can drive their trucks across the border, and a lot of them are doing a better job than people who sold through the Wheat Board.

TED ALLEN

In the last few years farmers have discovered that they can get a better price for grain in the United States than they can by selling to the Canadian Wheat Board in Canada. There are a number of reasons for this, but the bottom line is that we have a free trade agreement with the Americans and these farmers are discovering that by selling their wheat on their own they can get a much better return.

ALLAN JOHNSTON

So a number of farmers have challenged the Wheat Board and hauled their own grain and their neighbours' grain south to the States. And some of that grain the Wheat Board wouldn't even buy.

What were the repercussions when these farmers started to sell on their own?

JOHN DUVENAUD

The Wheat Board, having no means with which to enforce its monopoly, got Canada Customs to enforce it for them. Customs instituted a system of fines for farmers shipping wheat south without a permit and it's charged some of them.

ALLAN JOHNSTON

Canada Customs was stopping these guys and charging them under the Canada Customs Act. It's not as if they were trying to haul drugs across. These farmers are hauling wheat and barley, and it's their own wheat and barley for God's sake!

JIM PALLISTER

We're not talking about cocaine here. We're talking about wheat!

TED ALLEN

Most countries are concerned with what's coming into the country. It's only the old Soviet-style countries that are concerned with what's leaving the country. It's not as if wheat is some kind of state secret. It's a food product!

JOHN DUVENAUD

Canada Customs now controls three kinds of exports out of the country: endangered species, toxic waste and wheat. It's ludicrous.

JIM PALLISTER

When the Wheat Board was brought in we had 360,000 farms in Western Canada and now we have 125,000. It's not necessarily the Wheat Board that's responsible — surely we would have lost a lot of farms anyway — but is the loss partly because of those attitudes?

TED ALLEN

The Wheat Board needs to undergo major reforms. If it doesn't, it won't survive. And if it doesn't survive, the fault will lie with those who have insisted on the status quo.[1]

What are some of the other problems with the Wheat Board that concern you?

ALLAN JOHNSTON

One of my biggest beefs is that we ship our grain uncleaned to Thunder Bay and Vancouver. We ship it dirty, subsidized by the taxpayer, and then it's cleaned by union labour at $25 or $28 an hour. Then when a farmer needs feed grain for his livestock back in the Prairies, the freight's got to be paid and it's shipped back. As a result, the jobs for the processing and the cleaning, which should be here, are in Vancouver or Thunder Bay.

Why isn't the grain cleaned in the Prairies and then hauled out to Vancouver?

GRAHAM KEDGLEY

The reason the grain is cleaned out here in Vancouver is that the elevators are here. The elevators were built many years ago, and the grain could get out to them quickly then because there wasn't the volume. It could get cleaned quickly and be moved offshore. Now, with bigger volumes, the situation has changed, but unfortunately the system hasn't changed to cope with the problems.

The wheat pools have these big giants here — some people might call them dinosaurs — that they've spent a lot of money on and that they continue to spend a lot of money on. What would they do with them if the wheat was cleaned in the Prairies?

On the other hand, the elevators are also on prime waterfront land, and so there is an additional hidden cost in using them to clean grain.

JIM HARRIMAN

The Vancouver port has a lot of difficulties. It's on the inner harbour, which runs through the whole city. There is a lack of co-operation with pooling of stocks, so the average ship has to move at least three times to get a full load onboard. Labourers insist that if they work weekends they have to have overtime, and the end result is that we don't have a seven-day operation in the ports when we need it. Then there's the added problem of getting railcars to service our export sales.

GRAHAM KEDGLEY

One of our major problems is that railcars are taking 20 to 30 days to turn around and get back to the Prairies. As a result, when the grain gets to Vancouver, congestion caused by the equipment delays the cars getting back to take on more product. Railcars should be kept moving.

How important is the shipment of grain to the Port of Vancouver?

JOHN HODGE

Grain is the major commodity moving through the Port of Vancouver but it's a major problem getting the railcars turned around. Ship owners worry about their ships and how quickly they can turn them around. When the ships are moving they're making money. If they're sitting around doing nothing, they don't make any money at all. The ship owner's major concern is for the ship to come in, load, and get out as fast as possible.

In a perfect world a ship comes in from the sea, passes inspection, and is cleaned. Then it goes alongside, loads and sails. Hopefully we can do all of that in 36 or 48 hours. We've got a very efficient grain-loading system out here, once we get the grain.

But this is not a perfect world. A lot of things can go wrong. Bad weather on the Prairies will mean that the farmers can't get their grain into the elevators. A derailment will certainly set things back. A shortage of railcars has become very apparent during some seasons. And we've been known to have work stoppages in the harbour.

Meanwhile the ships are coming. You can't stop them and tell them to anchor in the middle of the ocean, so they just pile up here. A ship can wait three days, it can wait three weeks. Or in the worst scenario it can wait six weeks.

Who pays for the delay?

GRAHAM KEDGLEY

Demurrage is a charge that's levied by a ship when it arrives in port ready to accept product and the product isn't ready for it. The ship owner says, "Look, my ship's here, I want my money for sitting around in the sunshine." Those rates run from $8,000 to $10,000 a day for a decent-sized ship in Vancouver, so we are paying big sums of money to foreign shipping companies for the pleasure of having their ships sit in Vancouver harbour. Demurrage charges eventually come out of the pockets of the farmers and the rest of Canadian taxpayers.

JOHN HODGE

The bill for demurrage is sent to the Canadian Wheat Board but I have to assume that ultimately that cost will be deducted from the final price received by the farmers.

Is this kind of waiting game a common occurrence with other kinds of cargo?

No. With other products like logs and coal we get an extremely good turnaround. I can bring a container ship into this port and turn it easily within 36 hours and have a big load on it.

GRAHAM KEDGLEY

The coal train has a turnaround of seven days from the mine and back. The coal industry — and in fact all other bulk industries, sulphur or potash or whatever — have all gone to unit trains. These are trains that move in a block of 100, sometimes 110 cars, each car with 10,000 tons of product. The cars get locked together and never come apart. So the train leaves the mine and comes out here as a unit. It gets unloaded as a unit and it goes back as a unit. And it virtually never stops rolling.

But the grain system is totally different. You'll get a train made up of 20 cars of this and 10 cars of that, and then when it gets to the coast they'll put five cars into this siding and 20 cars into that elevator and it gets all jumbled up. The cars sit around and they get muddled up in the whole system and get shuffled around like a deck of cards. What we need are railcars running properly. They should be continually moving.

And we don't need more railcars. Please let's not see more railcars put into the system. All they would do is just clog it up more than it is now.

JIM HARRIMAN

The average turnaround for grain is 27 or 28 days, using three times more equipment than necessary. The taxpayer owns the bulk of the equipment, about 20,000 cars, and pays for the replacements that go into the fleet every year. The reason that the industry doesn't pay for this equipment is, first, because it doesn't have to and, second, because it's not allowed to.

In the best of all possible worlds, if we had total efficiency, we would only need about half the equipment that we have today. That isn't likely to happen, but that is sort of the utopia. One of the key problems is that the people who have all of the authority don't have any responsibility. We need to move to a situation where there is a commercial relationship between the railroads and the shipper so that if one or the other doesn't perform, each is financially and legally responsible to the other. Because of the Wheat Board system, the farmer pays all the costs.

The Wheat Board is controlling competition and in some cases eliminating competition. Competition brings options, choice, innovation and efficiency to the marketplace, whether it's for the farmer, the company or the end user. With the status quo these benefits don't happen.

NOTES

1.   When elections to the Canadian Wheat Board were held in January 1999, some farmers critical of the board were elected. As a result, the demands for change from within the board are growing, but those voices are still a minority and the anti–Wheat Board lobby is alive and well.

---------------------- CHAPTER 12 ----------------------

COWBOY-COUNTRY ATTITUDES

JOE BEWS
TOM LIVINGSTON
STAN WILSON

*During a welcome encounter with some ranchers in south-
ern Alberta, we heard another take on government subsidy. In the West there are vast differences in people's attitudes
toward the government's role in the economy. While the agricultural industry had been the recipient of massive amounts of
subsidy over the years, these cowboys, whose families tamed
the West and who continued to raise cattle and grow their own
feed, saw government involvement as a Faustian bargain.
These guys were mavericks, the exception to the rule. They
were confident, logical and realistic. They also had a great
sense of humour.*

— The Team

JOE BEWS

I've always considered myself a cowboy because I come from cowboy
country, but really I'm a food producer who produces beef for people
out there to enjoy.

And your industry is free from subsidies?

JOE BEWS

It is and I hope it stays that way. Our associations out here are strong, and there's a good lobby that keeps government out.

STAN WILSON

We're honestly quite amazed at how much influence we have, considering our numbers. We've opposed marketing boards and government intervention ever since day one because we know that government can't run things as well as we can, especially in Canada. That's been proven time after time. Whenever the government gets involved, industry becomes too inefficient.

TOM LIVINGSTON

We've got some classic examples. The Russian government has tried to farm since 1917, and people have consistently starved to death. The American government has tried to farm since 1934, with the advent of Roosevelt, and they've had a surplus. The point is that governments do not know how to farm.

STAN WILSON

If we wanted to predict what the market for our product would be, we'd have to look into the future about three years. We've never found anyone in the cattle business who could predict that, and we know damn sure that nobody in government could.

Have cattle ranchers been affected by grain subsidies?

STAN WILSON

We've had to compete against subsidized freight to acquire feed grain for our business. During the Second World War there was a program called Feed Freight Assistance, which encouraged the production of meat on the East Coast to supply our army and our allies with pork and beef. It allowed Western grain to be moved to the Maritimes much more cheaply than the actual cost. After the war the program wasn't removed, and it created a distortion since grain producers in the Maritimes got a subsidy as well.

When the Crow Rate was in effect, the Alberta government established a subsidy for the livestock industry to offset the detrimental effect of the

Crow Rate and Feed Freight Assistance. In other words, the Alberta taxpayer was subsidizing the beef producer in Alberta to counteract the federal government's subsidy to the grain producer in the Prairies.

We use the term "natural comparative advantage" in producing. We have the climate, the land and the expertise to raise cattle in the foothills of the Rocky Mountains. That's where all these things happen naturally. But when government intervenes, it moves that production away from where it's comparatively advantaged.

TOM LIVINGSTON

When cattle are worth a lot of money, we're going to produce a lot of cattle. When they're worth nothing, we'll cut the numbers back to suit ourselves. We don't want the government telling us how to do this.

STAN WILSON

I think we run our industry very efficiently in the open market. And remember, we're not confined to Canada. We've always had a continental market and an international market. In order to be competitive we have to have the flexibility to market our product as we want to.

What happens when you ignore natural comparative advantage?

TOM LIVINGSTON

When governments were more affluent and there was a little more money floating around, there were several instances of provincial governments subsidizing a cow/calf industry in their own province. In other words, they tried to buy an industry. Saskatchewan tried this in 1971.

In the late 1960s and early 1970s Saskatchewan was drowning in grain. So the provincial government, in its wisdom, decided that the province should have a livestock industry. The government was paying $250 a head for any cow that could walk down the gangplank off the truck. Cows were worth about $62 a head in Alberta, but they were worth $250 a head in Saskatchewan. So some ranchers in Alberta immediately rounded up all their cows from 12 years old on up and sent them to Saskatchewan.

Neighbours of mine got wealthy selling cows to Saskatchewan.

What happened?

Tom Livingston

Well, they turned the cows into the wheat piles in the fields. Now, if a cow overloads on wheat she'll die, which is what happened to quite a few of those cows!

The government tried to buy an industry and distort the natural advantage of the industry and it didn't work. The Saskatchewan government finally ran out of money. They lost a large share of the cow/calf industry and they lost quite a large share of their feed industry. The government got involved where it had no business being involved.

Do provincial boundaries also have an effect on your industry?

Tom Livingston

There are more provincial barriers to trade in Canada than there are to international trade. When the United States was put together they decided that no state could erect a barrier against products from another state. So there's been free trade in the U.S. In Canada we decided in our wisdom that each provincial government would be its own little fiefdom and we'd keep products from other provinces out. If you owned a farm in Alberta and a ranch in B.C., you couldn't put your own grain in your own truck and haul it to B.C. to feed your own cattle because there was a provincial boundary. And we wonder why the country's in trouble and why the country won't work. Well, that's one of the reasons.

Do wheat growers and other people involved in farming see guys like you in the livestock industry as renegades?

Stan Wilson

Well, in Alberta 70 percent of the ranchers now also produce grain, so that attitude is not as prevalent as it was back in the homestead era.

Tom Livingston

Western Canada and the western U.S. were settled primarily by livestock people. Farmers didn't come out here first. Cowboys, livestock producers, came into the West first and they moved west to escape the government domination and restrictions that were taking place on the eastern seaboard. So the West was populated by independent people who wanted to manage their own affairs.

JOE BEWS

The West was founded on that attitude. People were sick of the attitude down East, and they were sick of government involvement.

Now, I have to admit that the provincial government tempted me once. They had a growth program out. I could invest $4,500 and if I received less than five inches of rain from May to June, I could capitalize on about $75,000. I thought, "Oh boy, this is a pretty good investment. There's a good chance I could win." And I'll tell you what — the night before it was all over, it rained an inch and a half and I never got a dime.

The next morning I woke up and asked myself, "What kind of a food producer am I?" I mean, what a bad attitude to have. Here I was supposed to be raising food, and here I'm hoping that it wouldn't rain so I couldn't raise food but could then make a bundle from the government. That's a bad attitude. I've never filled out another form since. That was it for me. The government has tempted us; it tempts all groups and I'm glad it didn't catch us.

My ancestors came out here with that attitude. They came out here with a lot of personal pride in what they did and they didn't want any help. They did it on their own. And they wanted me to do the same thing.

CHAPTER 13

TIPPING THE SCALES

COLIN BEASLEY
DEANE CRABBE
BRIAN CROWLEY
ROBERT NIELSEN
CATHERINE SWIFT

> *P*erhaps *the promise of financial help as one of the conditions of Maritime participation in Confederation can be identified as the beginning of a dependence on Ottawa in this part of the country. The propping up of SYSCO to the tune of more than $2 billion is the most famous example of this dependency. The three examples we use here occurred in the Maritimes, but the results of this kind of giveaway can be seen from coast to coast.*
>
> — The Team

CATHERINE SWIFT

One of the key problems with subsidies is that you end up making one player better off at the expense of another. And if you're in a market and you see your principal competitors get handed what will probably amount to their profit margin for that year, it's pretty clear what's going to happen in the marketplace. You're dead in the water. You're going to be a lot worse off.

Forestry in New Brunswick

DEANE CRABBE

Forestry's a big business here in New Brunswick. We have about 15 million acres of forest lands. We're handy to sea transportation and we're well situated for the northeastern U.S. market, so I guess it's natural that it's the biggest industry we have in this province.

The pulp and paper industry in Canada has gone through some pretty hard times in the last few years, and there's been a lot of government assistance available to those who wanted it. I've seen so many cases where government, by coaxing people to take its money, made it more difficult for other people who were in the same business.

Ottawa gave, I'm not talking about millions, I'm talking about billions of dollars to companies that went into the forests in Alberta and built monstrous pulp mills. It made the rest of the industry sick and some of the mills have had to close. So what did you gain by starting a development in one area that put what had already been developed in another area out of business? When you flood the market, somebody is going to have to pay the price.

Down in Nova Scotia the government spent $4 million or $5 million to build a furniture factory in competition with another business that had been making furniture for years. Now they're both closed. If the government had stayed out of it, the other operation would still be in business.

There are all kinds of horror stories like these. We've seen so many instances where government has taken millions and millions of taxpayers' dollars and the money has been completely wasted. The government has a whole lot of employees with a whole lot of education and no practical experience, and these people don't make very good judgment calls.

Did you ever ask the government for assistance?

DEANE CRABBE

We took a subsidy one time, over 20 years ago, for a change to our planing mill. Our accountants said, "You're foolish not to take it because if you don't take it, somebody else will." So we gave in and we've been sorry ever since. The subsidy was for $110,000. After we spent $85,000 of it we had a discussion and said, "That's enough of that. We shouldn't have taken it in the first place." And that was it. It kind of went against our grain, so to speak. We could have survived without it.

Maritime Motels

ROBERT NIELSEN

About 30 miles north of here, near Grand Falls, New Brunswick, is a quite good-quality motel complex called Près du Lac, which was built with the help of very substantial government money. Then someone proposed building a place called Lakeside Lodge a little south of Grand Falls, within 15 miles of Près du Lac. Now, I can tell you, Victoria County is not a great magnet for conventions or conferences or things like that. The total population of the county is only about 18,000 or 20,000. But somebody had the idea that they were going to attract Americans over to Lakeside Lodge, although the lake is more of an overgrown pond than a lake.

They built quite a glossy building, done with grants from the federal government and the provincial Tourism Department and perhaps some bank loans. The place went belly-up after a year and a half.

If it had succeeded, it would have taken business away from the other government-assisted resort. It made no sense to build these two quite similar facilities so close together in an area of small population where they couldn't possibly attract enough tourists.

A similar thing happened in Cape Breton. The existing hotels and motels in Sydney were encouraged to expand and were offered grants, or loans on favourable terms. Other hotel chains not in the region were also invited to open operations there. And so from 1985 to 1990 the number of hotel rooms in Sydney doubled from 500 to nearly 1,000.

As a result, the hotels all started going broke because Sydney, let's face it, is not a mecca for conventioneers or pleasure seekers. So for, say, $30 million, the area got a temporary boom in the building trades, but the long-term effect was that the hotels and motels in Sydney were on their uppers.[1]

International Wallcoverings, Brampton, Ontario

COLIN BEASLEY

Between 1982 and 1988 the wallpaper industry in North America was tremendously successful and profitable. People made an awful lot of money, but the seeds of what happened in 1989 were sown in that period. Because people were putting out the same boring products year after year, they lost sight of the fact that it is a creative industry where design and colour are very important.

Inevitably the downturn happened, and by 1989 a lot of companies were closing or shutting down plants. People were being laid off. The industry was beginning to go through a complete restructuring and rationalization, and we were very concerned about the future. It was obviously not the environment in which to set up another wallpaper manufacturer. Not that we resented competition, but we were concerned about subsidized competition.

When we heard that St. Clair Paint and Paper had decided to open Cape Breton Wallcoverings and saw that the management team had been put in place and equipment was being bought, we certainly felt that it wouldn't last — not unless the government was prepared to keep on subsidizing it.

What were the major difficulties for the new wallpaper company in a place like Cape Breton?

COLIN BEASLEY

The principal difficulty was getting the right creative skills and talent there. In this part of Ontario there are six established companies. There are also engraving companies here and book-binding companies. There are ink suppliers and designers. Why go to Cape Breton when St. Clair could have set the company up here, where we have 20 to 25 percent of the U.S. market, as well as a big share of the Canadian market?

What was the effect of this new enterprise on International Wallcoverings?

COLIN BEASLEY

It took away our business in two ways. First of all, because St. Clair had a captive manufacturer, it put more of that product in its stores and replaced some of our product and the products of other suppliers. That was the direct effect. And indirectly they contract-manufactured for a number of other people in the industry while we were also contract-manufacturing for these people. They were selling wallpaper for approximately 25 percent below our price and they were managing to do so for two reasons: because of the subsidies and because they were selling at a loss. We lost, directly or indirectly, $2 million to $3 million a year for three years and we laid off between 12 and 15 people.

The key point is that without subsidies, this plant would never have been set up at all.

What happened to the company?

COLIN BEASLEY

Cape Breton Wallcoverings went into receivership in 1991. Since then the industry has gone through a rationalization and restructuring. It awoke to the fact that it involves colour and design and creative activity. The products put out today are spectacular. So the market is growing again and we are very successful and highly profitable now.

Do you accept any subsidies?

COLIN BEASLEY

International Wallcoverings accepts training grants and we're also going to receive a grant toward our new computer system. I'll be quite honest with you: I feel I have a responsibility as a director of a public company to take advantage of whatever is there. But I wish the subsidies were not there.

BRIAN CROWLEY

Once the government creates a system in which people can ask for subsidies and get them, everyone will ask for them. If you are in business and you see your competitor get some kind of competitive advantage, you are going to seek the same advantage. It doesn't matter whether the competitive advantage is access to cheaper capital, access to better-trained workers or access to government grants, if your competitors have it, you cannot afford not to pursue it. And indeed you should. It's a perfectly rational thing to do.

We also have a system in which successful businesses often can't get support from government because they're too successful, but they are taxed so highly that the tax money that comes from them goes to subsidize their competitors who are less successful. We have a system in Atlantic Canada in which weaker companies are rewarded and supported by government at the expense of more successful companies. There's a perverse kind of incentive at work here.

NOTES

1. "Uppers" is a Maritime expression meaning "in trouble" or "desperate."

110

CHAPTER 14

FISHING FOR DOLLARS

MILLER AYRE
SHANNON CONWAY
MURRAY COOLICAN
PARZIVAL COPES
ROBERT GREENWOOD

DIANE KEOUGH
MICHAEL MACDONALD
CHARLIE MCMILLAN
JENNIFER SMITH
RON WHYNACHT

A lthough the crisis in the fishing industry, which began to make news in the early 1990s, seemed to focus mostly on Newfoundland, it became clear to us as we travelled down East that the effect was devastating throughout the region. For decades the Atlantic fishery had been the recipient of infusions of capital and job-creation plans at both the federal and provincial levels. The importance of the federal government in regulating the day-to-day lives of fishermen was one of the reasons Newfoundlanders focused their anger on Ottawa when the federal minister of fisheries announced a moratorium on cod fishing in 1992.

Since we recorded our conversations about the industry on the East Coast, similar problems have arisen in British Columbia with the West Coast ground fishery. In 1999 the auditor general of Canada warned that the shellfish industry, until now presumed to be in good shape, would face similar trouble in the near future if problems were not addressed ... and soon.

— The Team

JENNIFER SMITH

My earliest memories are of fishermen saying, "The fishery isn't what it used to be. There's a problem. There aren't as many fish as there used to be. There's something wrong," and politicians saying, "No, it's just that the water's too cold this year, or the water's too warm this year, it's this, it's that, but it's not a big problem." If we had listened to the fishermen 15 or 20 years ago, we wouldn't have the crisis we do now.[1]

MILLER AYRE

Our fish are depleted. This is a devastating reality for Newfoundland, and it makes for a big problem. It's like no auto industry in Ontario, no wheat in Saskatchewan, no oil in Alberta, no Asia–Pacific for B.C.

MICHAEL MACDONALD

All Canadians should understand that the decline of the Atlantic fishery is one of the worst tragedies in the history of our country. We had one of the richest fisheries in the world and we've lost it.

Do you know what happened to the cod?

RON WHYNACHT

It's not clear what the single biggest cause of the cod depletion was, whether the fish were caught or moved or failed to reproduce because of the environment, but the most popular theory is that it was a combination of several factors, including overharvesting, the environment and the predator-prey relationship.

MICHAEL MACDONALD

There are a whole myriad of reasons why it happened and overfishing is one of them. One of the issues we have to face is that for over 20 years the government used the fishery as a way of implementing a social policy. Basically it encouraged the development of fish-processing facilities and small fisheries in communities all along the coastline. Had these industries been the result of market development, they would have survived. But as soon as the resources shrank, the communities collapsed.

MURRAY COOLICAN

There were subsidies to people to build small fish plants and subsidies to people to buy bigger boats that could catch more fish. But you also had the federal fisheries minister trying to reduce the number of small fish being caught; at the same time the subsidy department was

112

providing money to small fish-plant owners to buy new equipment that would allow them to process smaller and smaller fish. There was even a program in which the federal government was encouraging fishermen to build their own fish plants so they could take their fish to the plants that they owned. But the government was still subsidizing some of the large fish companies to build new plants as well. It didn't make any sense.

A modern plant in Lockport, Nova Scotia, was built in the late 1970s. The reason it had to close was that it couldn't get fish from the inshore fishermen anymore because they were taking their fish to their own fish plants, which had been built with subsidies from the same government that had subsidized Lockport! We wound up with an overcapacity of fish plants, which created too much demand on the fishery. A lot of those plants are now closed.

All of these factors resulted in too much pressure on the fish stocks and the collapse of the groundfish fishery. Without those subsidies perhaps we could still have a viable fishery here.

What was the effect on the fishing communities?

RON WHYNACHT

The fishermen had no fish to catch so their boats stayed in port. There weren't enough fish to process so the processing plants started closing. A lot of social and community problems started to develop. How were people going to live? Where were they going to go? Many of the people in the fishery were not trained and did not have the skills to do a lot of jobs other than fishing and processing fish. In many of the rural communities the hardship was unbelievable.

What was the effect of the downturn on companies like National Sea Products?

RON WHYNACHT

The collapse of the fishery in the late 1980s caused the whole industry to rethink itself. We had debts in excess of $100 million from the expansion in the 1980s when the fishery was quite healthy and the industry was still growing. Ships were being built, plants were being built, and we were very much in an expansionary mode.

We had to financially restructure our business and sell off many of our foreign operations. We went from about 7,500 employees down to about 1,200. We're still striving to find a solution that works but I don't think financial support from the government is going to provide that. We have to find a better way.

JENNIFER SMITH

I'm from rural Newfoundland. There are people in my family who are fishermen. My brother-in-law is currently on "the package," the TAGS program.[2] I don't think anybody quite realizes how many people in this province suffer because they can't make a living for themselves and have to accept payments from Ottawa. It's very demoralizing for people who have earned a living their entire lives.

PARZIVAL COPES

The problem I see with the Newfoundland economy and the Newfoundland fishery is that there are two conventional wisdoms that have been held here for too long.

The first one is that Newfoundlanders have considered it a matter of birthright that anyone who wants to become a fisherman should be able to go into the fishery, and that it is the obligation of government to see to it that people can make a decent living in the fishery. And at one time, of course, that was precisely how Newfoundland operated. The one big industry was the fishing industry and the population was small enough and the resource was large enough in relation to the population that there was no reason to keep people out of the fishery. It's an entirely different matter now. The population has expanded enormously. Technology has improved so that you need far fewer fishers and far fewer boats to catch the same amount of fish. If you want to keep up with the competition — the Icelanders, for instance — you have to use the technology that is going to be efficient. When the fishing industry was closed down, we had three or four times as many boats and people as were needed to run an efficient industry.

The second conventional wisdom is that the greatest assets of the province are the people of the province. "Our greatest assets are our people," Joey Smallwood said.[3] And the conclusion drawn from that was that we should discourage emigration from Newfoundland. Joey Smallwood negotiated with the federal government for all kinds of support for the Newfoundland economy but the one thing he was adamant about was that there was to be no more money to move people out of the province. They had to stay in Newfoundland.

When the government had a resettlement program, he would take the unemployed or underemployed people from the smaller outports and move them to larger places, but he was just reshuffling the unemployed. In many cases they ended up in welfare ghettos where there was no work available at all. Not a penny was spent on moving people to places where there were jobs. Thirty years ago there were plenty of jobs on the mainland. We had plenty of opportunities and those opportunities were missed. So as far as the greatest asset to the province being its people is concerned, it was an asset that was going to waste.

What were your answers for the problems you identified in the 1960s?

PARZIVAL COPES

We made specific recommendations in *St. John's and Newfoundland — An Economic Survey* to rationalize the fishing industry, to reduce the labour force by at least half and to reduce the number of vessels. Far too many boats were being used. Far too much was being spent on gear and equipment that was not needed. We could have had a far more productive fishery if it was a great deal smaller because we could still catch the same amount of fish, but we could do it with fewer people and with fewer boats. The catch per fisher and per boat would be greatly increased. We could have had a viable fishing industry that would not have to be subsidized.

However, the major problem in Newfoundland was high unemployment. Even with all those excessive numbers in the fishery, we still had 20 percent unemployment. If we reduced the fishing industry, the major employer, we would have had to reduce the number of people working there by one-half to two-thirds. What were the prospects for those people when we had so much unemployment already?

The logical consequence that could not be avoided was that we had to do something about mopping up the unemployment. I knew there was no way that we were going to employ all of those people. So we had to look at it from the other end as well: labour mobility. We had to help people get jobs where there were jobs. And in those days there were jobs on the mainland.

115

I emphasized that there was no reason that people who were adventurously inclined should not go and look for jobs elsewhere and relieve the pressure of the unemployment situation in Newfoundland. At the same time I suggested the exploration of additional opportunities for employment at home. But the problem with the Newfoundland government at the time was that it wanted to create more jobs in Newfoundland. In other words, to bring jobs to the people. So the conventional wisdom that our people are our greatest asset and that we should keep them in the province held until very recently.

MILLER AYRE

There's always an assumption somewhere along the line that there's an answer. I doubt that Smallwood knew what the answer was and steadfastly refused to put it into effect. I don't think that when he handed the reins over to Frank Moores he said, "By the way, Frank, I know what the answer is and it's in the bottom drawer, but just don't ever look at it and for heaven's sake, don't apply it." And then Moores said it to Peckford, and Peckford said it to Wells and so on. It's not as though somebody in government knows the answers to the problems of Newfoundland's economy. Simple as that![4]

ROBERT GREENWOOD

What really screwed things up was when the unemployment system was extended to the fishery in the 1970s. The number of fishermen greatly increased then because they could fish for part of the year and collect unemployment insurance the rest of the time.

MICHAEL MACDONALD

Newfoundland came reluctantly into Confederation when Joey Smallwood promised Newfoundlanders the baby bonus and several other cheques from Ottawa. It was only after that event that Smallwood got the federal government to put the fishery in the unemployment cycle. And that was the beginning of the end.

PARZIVAL COPES

What this meant was that it was no longer an insurance scheme against an unlikely and unfortunate contingency; it was a payout that was guaranteed during the winter. It became a massive subsidy and as a result an enormous amount of government funding went into the fishing industry.

At the same time, the government was trying to put more and more people into the fishing industry because it was the only place that could

116

accommodate people in the economy. The reason they could do that is that fishing is an open-access resource. Since nobody owns the fish resource, anybody can get a small boat and start dipping into the pool of fish. The result was that the fishing industry essentially became an employer of last resort. If you couldn't get a job elsewhere, you could go and work in the fishery. So the industry became overloaded with people.

If you compared ours with other more productive fishing economies, like Iceland's, you would find that 4,000 or 5,000 of its fishermen would catch more than twice as much as the Newfoundlanders, whose numbers at times rose to 30,000. It really was a scandalous waste of public resources to overexploit the fishing industry!

MURRAY COOLICAN

Over the 15 years following the introduction of unemployment insurance into the industry, there was, I think, an increase of 10,000 people in the fishery in Atlantic Canada — not because there were enough fish out there or because it was an efficient business; it was simply because of government subsidies and the introduction of unemployment insurance.

ROBERT GREENWOOD

Once people had their stamps and qualified for unemployment insurance, they were better off to quit because if they worked and made more money, they would collect less money later on.

There were no incentives to work for those extra weeks if work were available, or to enhance entrepreneurship or enhance their education. That's one of the big problems in the fishery. People didn't need to finish high school to make a very good living and have a very good quality of life. I heard of a 19-year-old student who was almost finished a technical degree and he quit. The principal said, "You're nuts. There's opportunity for you to have options and to make money." And the kid said, "Look, I'm going into the shrimp fishery. I'm going to make more in two months than you're gonna make all year." What do you say to a kid who has an opportunity to make good money for two months and then collect unemployment insurance? He'd be a fool not to do it.

MICHAEL MACDONALD

The really diabolical effect was that in a typical fishing community where people had been seasonal workers for perhaps 400 years, the whole culture and their whole way of life was built on this. Fishermen would work

117

the fishery, then return home and spend the other months logging, farming, repairing houses, or repairing their boats and mending their nets.

With unemployment insurance they worked their 12 or 14 weeks and then it was over, and a coherent annual cycle of culture and economy and life collapsed.

And that is a terrible thing.

MURRAY COOLICAN

There's a perception in the rest of Canada that the entire fishery is closed down, that you shouldn't eat fish because it is possibly the last one you're ever going to get. Well, it's not the case. There still is a good fishery. It's not necessarily in groundfish, but in lobster and scallops and that sort of thing. Some people in the fishery earn a very good living, $100,000 or $150,000 a year, and then at the end of the season, go on unemployment. And they do it quite legally. It's within the system.

PARZIVAL COPES

If you put together all the subsidies and payments made to the fishery by two levels of government, provincial and federal, there were years in which the amount of money spent was in excess of the value of the catch, and far in excess of the income made by fishermen. Now, that is subsidizing an industry more than 100 percent. That is not sustainable, and look where we've ended up now.

MURRAY COOLICAN

What the government has done, through a combination of unemployment insurance and subsidies to the fishery, is create a dependence on something that is not economic.

Since the crisis began, have government attitudes been changing?

ROBERT GREENWOOD

I've recently seen people from government agencies — federal, provincial and municipal — sit down at the same table and talk about issues. These people deal with the same stuff day in, day out, but have never met each other before. Now they are being forced to meet because of fiscal restraint and the crisis we're in.

118

CHARLIE MCMILLAN

The cost of all of this is just too high simply because of the duplication in the bureaucracies of the federal, provincial and the regional governments. And the conflicts between and within the provincial and federal governments have slowed the industry down.

Let me give you an example. Brian Tobin, who was the minister of fisheries in 1995, pointed out that the Norwegians have a huge coast, and yet 40 percent of the fish in Norway come from aquaculture, a high-technology industry. What's happening in Canada? Tobin openly said his bureaucrats in the Department of Fisheries were against aquaculture. It's a new form of business, a new form of technology, but they preferred the traditional fisheries.

ROBERT GREENWOOD

But there are now some aquaculture industries opening up. With the decline in the traditional harvesting sector we need to harvest more fish by raising it ourselves. Some people are even trying to farm cod now.

What was the effect of this crisis on young people in Newfoundland?

DIANE KEOUGH

Many of the young people who come from fishing families have realized that what their parents did for a living will not be possible for them. When they were growing up the fishery was their mainstay. Now their parents are out of work and they're asking where that leaves them. They thought the fishing industry would provide them with a job and now it won't. So what's next?

SHANNON CONWAY

A lot of Newfoundland teenagers believe they can go through high school and perhaps university, but once they have their education there'll be no jobs here.

A lot of them feel that they're going to have to move away and a lot of them feel that they just don't have a choice. We're trying to give them a choice. We let them know that there are things out there: the tourism industry, aquaculture and so on. We're trying to convince young people that they will be able to move away from the old economy, that they do have a future in Newfoundland.

MILLER AYRE

There are still opportunities to catch certain species that are not affected by the moratorium because they're not at risk. You may opt to go after something that is not a traditional fishing activity but remain a fisherman or a fisherwoman. If you're a young adult with no capital, however, you're more likely to move.

Your parents, on the other hand, own their home. They have a boat. They have a car. They have everything here. If they try to move from a small village, they're going to sell the house for next to nothing, and they're going to end up in Toronto living in a basement apartment, trying to start their life over again. That option, I suggest, is really not on.

The horrible part is that the only people for whom migration is a real possibility are the young people, and migration may create serious problems in terms of developing the economy over time.

What's the next step in solving the problems of the fishery?

CHARLIE MCMILLAN

We have the Department of Fisheries and Oceans in Ottawa, where there are no fish, except maybe in the odd little lake. But we do have the two coastal fisheries. Why don't we just get rid of the Department of Fisheries and set up agencies on the East Coast and on the West Coast and dismantle the massive bureaucracy in Ottawa?

If, 20 years ago, the Department of Fisheries had planned to mismanage the fisheries, they couldn't have done a better job![5]

NOTES

1. The moratorium on cod fishing was announced by the Mulroney government in 1992.
2. The Atlantic Groundfish Strategy, allocated $1.9 billion by the government, was in effect from May 16, 1994, to August 29, 1998, to assist those affected by the groundfish moratorium.
3. Joseph R. Smallwood was the Liberal premier of Newfoundland from 1949, when the province joined Confederation, to 1972.

4. Premiers after Smallwod: Frank Moores (PC) 1972–1979; Brian Peckford (PC) 1979–1989; Clyde Wells (Lib) 1989–1996; Brian Tobin (Lib) 1996–2000. Roger Grimes is the current premier.

5. The 1999 Report of the Auditor General of Canada suggested that many of the problems associated with the Department of Fisheries and Oceans management of the Atlantic groundfish fishery also exist in the department's management of the Atlantic shellfish fisheries. The report pointed specifically to the weaknesses in the department's approach to co-management, which would allow participants to assume greater responsibility for their industry. This is an important element of sustainability. The department's response to the criticism did not indicate an intention to take action to address the issue of co-management.

CHAPTER 15

THE POLITICS OF THE DOLE

BRIAN CROWLEY
LLOYD FRANCIS
JOHN ELDON GREEN
MICHAEL MACDONALD
CHARLIE MCMILLAN

*W*e *haven't quite figured out why the federal government changed the name of one of the safety net programs from Unemployment Insurance to Employment Insurance in 1996. UI seems pretty clear to us: insurance against the possibility of unemployment, right? Well, isn't employment insurance just the opposite? Insurance against the possibility of employment? This decision makes no sense to us, so we'll continue to call it UI.*

When we heard about the changes that took place in the UI program in the early 1970s, we began to understand the motives of many government decisions and the resulting plight, not only of Atlantic fishermen, but of millions of workers in many other industries across the country. We realized that politicians really believe they can create jobs!

— The Team

LLOYD FRANCIS

Until the early 1970s unemployment insurance was an insurance scheme designed on fairly conventional social insurance principles. But then in 1974 Bryce Mackasey, the minister of labour, decided to extend unemployment insurance to seasonal workers. The question was, who was a seasonal worker?

He talked to the Atlantic caucus and they were all in favour of fishermen being seasonal. He spoke to others and they were in favour of forestry being seasonal. He wasn't that quick to take on agricultural workers but eventually, after lobbying efforts, they also became seasonal. One after another, they all got in.

The chairman of the Unemployment Insurance Commission was Clifford Murcheson from Saskatchewan.[1]

He was a very rugged individual whose integrity was beyond reproach. He had grave misgivings about what was being proposed. He advised his minister that it was wrong. He recommended not to do it.

First of all, he warned, it would be a permanent subsidy to seasonal industry. It would keep too many people in seasonal employment. It was also a regional welfare transfer, a transfer from central areas with high employment to other areas with low employment, and it would add enormously to the deficit of the program. Everything Murcheson said turned out to be true, but at the time he couldn't get anywhere with his minister. Mackasey paid no attention to his representations. Clifford came to me and I went over his memos. Then I went on the committee studying the revisions. When I told the committee that I thought the changes would destroy the fund over a period of time, the chairman of the committee, who is a good friend to this day, took me aside and said, "Lloyd, you're not being very helpful. Suppose you get off the committee." And I was taken off the committee. I don't think there was any member or any Cabinet minister who gave me more than the time of day. They all thought it was a great idea. Mackasey did a very effective lobby on the caucus and no one could possibly counter him. The fact was that the proposal was also immensely popular with a large number of elected representatives and Mackasey was in favour of Santa Claus, so there was nothing anyone could do to stop it.

Bryce Mackasey destroyed unemployment insurance. When he brought in the fishermen, the forestry workers and eventually the agricultural workers, it became a regional transfer of welfare funds. If it was a welfare program, it should have been handled within a welfare context. By including these people it also provided a permanent subsidy to seasonal industries and to seasonal employers by retaining more people in those jobs than should have stayed in them. These people should have shifted to other kinds of employment. Not easily done, I know, but in the long-term interests of the country it had to be done. The program became a boondoggle from that point on. Abuses crept in and now we have a situation that will be very hard to correct.

CHARLIE MCMILLAN

The difficulty is that once people get on unemployment insurance they can't get off. If you go down to parts of Atlantic Canada, eastern Quebec, parts of Ontario, the only person who goes out in the morning is the kid who's going to school. The parents and grandparents aren't going out to jobs because they're getting unemployment insurance. We're building second- and third-generation dependency families, all requiring government assistance through UI and other forms of government policy.

BRIAN CROWLEY

With unemployment insurance the trend was upward even during the boom years of the 1980s. After the recession at the beginning of the 1980s, we enjoyed six or seven years of really stellar economic growth, but the number of unemployment beneficiaries continued to go up. We have created a system in which it is easy for people to drop out of the productive economy.

I'm not saying, by the way, that those people are lazy, or that they're welfare bums. Those people are responding entirely rationally to a set of incentives that we have put into place. If you are a fish-plant worker in Newfoundland and there are hundreds of people in your village, but only 40 or 50 jobs in your local fish plant, it makes perfect sense for the community to get together and parcel out those jobs in 10-week slices because once you work for 10 weeks, your income is guaranteed for the rest of the year. We have created an incentive system for communities to look after themselves at the expense of other workers in other kinds of industries.

I don't blame these people for doing that. I think the systems were put into place with the best of intentions, but they were bad systems. We cannot as a society afford to pay people who are able to be part of the productive economy not to participate in it.

CHARLIE MCMILLAN

Some provincial governments, including the Joe Ghiz government in Prince Edward Island, my home province, had a political strategy of hiring people for 10 weeks through the provincial government and its various agencies.[2] Those 10 weeks allowed individuals to get their unemployment stamps. Then they would be laid off and other people would be hired, including some of their relatives. Since the unemployment insurance was federal, the provincial government could ratchet up spending and turn it over to the government in Ottawa.

MICHAEL MACDONALD

With unemployment insurance, the economy will build itself around the system. Here's an example: the autumn months are three of the finest months in Nova Scotia, but we have great difficulties in Cape Breton in extending the tourism season into September, October and November because the motel and hotel owners have trouble getting people who already have their stamps to work. The economy has followed the line of least resistance.

But I should tell you that I don't find unemployment insurance to be a moral problem, although I know a lot of bureaucrats do. If Maritimers or Albertans or people in northern Ontario have been able to use the system for their own advantage, that's very entrepreneurial. They didn't design the system, but they know how to use it, and I'm very optimistic about that.

JOHN ELDON GREEN

I get very annoyed at some of these critics who are constantly commenting on all of these people who want to lay back and draw unemployment. I live among these people here on Prince Edward Island. They don't have to be teased to go back to work. They don't have to be bribed to go back to work. They would rather do anything than draw unemployment. That is a misunderstanding people in government have as well.

What do you think of the claim by governments that they can establish employment opportunities around the country?

JOHN ELDON GREEN

I have a story. I was at the premiers' conference, with our premier, when the premiers all agreed that the thing the governments should all be doing now is creating jobs. That would be the new initiative right across the country. At the break I turned to our premier and said, "I have a little problem with that, Premier. When you go back to P.E.I. you're going to turn to people like me and say, 'We'd like you to start creating jobs.' And I have to tell you that if I was any good at creating jobs, I wouldn't be working for you. I'd be out there making money creating jobs." He said that there are other people in the economic development sector who had different gifts and he presumed that they would be able to create jobs. So I said, "OK, Premier, that begs the question: if they are so good at creating jobs, why are they working for you? Why aren't they out there creating jobs? I have to say they're not very smart because they could be out creating jobs and here they are working for you." The premier turned and walked away and that was the end of the conversation.

Government should be in the business of creating government jobs. It does a very good job of that. But for 25 years I've watched the federal government's initiative to generate jobs for the economy, and I've seen young people hired straight out of university whose mandate was to create jobs. I wondered how it was going to work. And 25 years later I'm still wondering.

Who creates jobs, then?

JOHN ELDON GREEN

Jobs are created by the risk takers, by the entrepreneurs, by the gamblers.

NOTES

1. The Unemployment Insurance Commission was established in 1941. The name was changed to the Canada Employment Insurance Commission in 1996.
2. Joseph A. Ghiz was Liberal premier of P.E.I. from 1986 to 1993.

CHAPTER 16

THE REGIONAL DEVELOPMENT
SWEEPSTAKES

MILLER AYRE
PARZIVAL COPES
DEANE CRABBE
MICHAEL MACDONALD

TOM MCMILLAN
ROBERT NIELSEN
DONALD SAVOIE

For a long time people have referred to regional economic disparities in terms of the "have" and the "have-not" provinces. But one person we interviewed in Nova Scotia took umbrage when we referred to Nova Scotia as one of the latter and asked us, "Have not what?" We hesitated and asked ourselves the same question, and then began to see Atlantic Canada from a new perspective.

Ottawa has always treated regions far away from the capital as outlying areas and the people living there as country cousins: quaint but in need of nurturing and guidance from the city folk.

The stories we heard of regional development handouts across the country astonished us and provided some of the most compelling insights of our entire journey.

— The Team

MICHAEL MACDONALD

When I was a kid my grandfather used to tell me, "The railway doesn't run from Vancouver to Halifax; it runs from Halifax to Toronto and from Vancouver to Toronto." Well, that's how Canada works.

MILLER AYRE

Canada has steadfastly maintained a growth program for the centre of the country, but not for the hinterland. Consequently, any province not part of that central mentality has been the beneficiary of a form of regional development. Now, regional development has never worked, and no one can really find answers to the question of what a federal government should be doing to develop the economy of Newfoundland or anywhere else.

PARZIVAL COPES

With subsidies from Ottawa, Joey Smallwood started up a dozen new industries, manufacturing things from batteries to rubber boots. The market was much too small and these industries were too far away from the main markets and they all failed. There was a misapplication of subsidies to industries that didn't have a chance of making it. But with a little bit of insight that could have been perceived ahead of time.

MICHAEL MACDONALD

Regional development is really one of the big insights into how Canada works. If you look at the history of all of these agencies and initiatives and all of these federal programs, it's not cynical to conclude that the Government of Canada is not in the economic development business; it's in the dependency business. Economic development means independence. It means power to the regions. And that hasn't happened in Canada.

What were the reasons for the first regional development programs?

DONALD SAVOIE

We have to go back to the 1960s when Pierre Trudeau was talking about a "Just Society." He felt there were two main problems in this country — language and the poor regions — and he set out to solve both. He appointed his most trusted advisor, Jean Marchand, to lead the charge, and they initially focused exclusively on Atlantic Canada and eastern Quebec, the Gaspé and Lac-St.-Jean, because that's where the real problems were. But over the years regional development got pushed and pulled to every nook and cranny of the country because the politics really came into play. Late in the 1960s and early in 1970 we had the FLQ crisis and the growing separatism problem.[1] A lot of people in Quebec started to make the case that if regional development was going to be tied to a growth pole — because back then that was the key; you looked at urban centres and said let's build on these, Halifax, Moncton and so on — as our growth pole is the city of Montreal, regional development should apply there.

But once the federal Cabinet said, "OK, let's supply some of these programs to the City of Montreal," it opened a floodgate, and the effects
reached all the way to Vancouver. Even the ski resort at Whistler was a
regional development project, partially financed at the time by the
Department of Regional Economic Expansion (DREE).

From then on MPs from all over could go back home and say, "Look
what I've done. I've been able to get our city, our urban area, our
towns designated."

Once the City of Montreal was tagged, anybody with any claim could
knock on the door. One thing that motivates most politicians is visibility. If they can go back home and say, "I've done this," it's a hell of a
coup. And so regional development became part of politics.

TOM MCMILLAN

DREE was established in 1969 by the Trudeau government to help eliminate or at least alleviate regional disparities across the country, that is
to say, to narrow the gap in income and job opportunities between have
and have-not areas. However, while regional development began with
that rationale, over the years it became a honey pot for practically every
part of the country, whatever its job levels or per capita income. In my
time as a minister, my fellow Cabinet ministers and I were party to decisions that were granting millions of dollars to wealthy parts of the country just as much as to small and poor areas.

We were doling out millions of dollars in the name of regional development
and job creation to entrepreneurs and enterprises, small, medium and
large, right across the country, from one end of the continent to the other.

DONALD SAVOIE

At the height of it in 1983 Ed Lumley, who was appointed to oversee
regional development (I think at the time DREE had been abolished and
it was now DRIE, the Department of Regional Industrial Expansion), got
up in the House of Commons and said, "I have good news. I have new
regional programming that applies in every city, every town, every community, Toronto included." So finally we had a regional program that
every member of the House could agree on because it applied to every
riding, and from there we've never been able to go back. When Brian
Mulroney came into office in 1984 he was under a lot of pressure from
people on the East Coast who said that this national program was

nonsense and the whole thing should be scrapped. Bear in mind that in the mid-1980s the Ontario economy was booming but the East Coast was in really bad shape. It hadn't recovered from the massive recession of the early 1980s, and the premiers in the Atlantic provinces said that this approach to regional development didn't make any sense at all.

In one case somebody had applied for a grant to make potato chips in Hamilton or in Nova Scotia. He applied in both places. And lo and behold, the offer was more generous in Hamilton. The premiers felt that if regional programming meant that a firm could get more assistance to make potato chips by going to Hamilton than by going to Nova Scotia, then the whole thing should be cut.

Mulroney came back to Ottawa after meetings in the Maritimes, and John Crosbie got after him and said they had to do something about this situation. So the Mulroney government decided to scrap the existing programs. Instead they established a Department of Industry which would look at all of Canada, and they introduced a patchwork of programs for different regions. The first one was the Atlantic Canada Opportunities Agency (ACOA). They gave it $1.8 billion. Within three weeks Don Mazankowski, who was the senior minister from the West, said, "We need one in Western Canada, too." So there was a new Western agency, Western Economic Diversification (WED), with a budget of $1.1 billion. And then the province of Quebec said, "If it's good enough for the East Coast, we need one here as well." So they got the Federal Office for Regional Development in Quebec (FORD-Q), with a budget of a billion-plus.

What it became was a bastardization of regional policy, where one community in a province was in competition with the next one.

TOM MCMILLAN

ACOA was supposed to be an entirely different approach to regional development. Instead of having non–Atlantic Canadian bureaucrats ensconced in Ottawa making decisions by remote control for the benefit of Atlantic Canada, ACOA was supposed to be rooted in the region. Its headquarters were in Moncton and the bureaucrats were to be resident there. Preferably the minister responsible for ACOA was to be an Atlantic Canadian, but this wasn't always the case. The bureaucrats and politicians were to be advised by real live, warmblooded entrepreneurs from within the region with real on-the-ground experience in the private sector. It was to be a completely different way of creating wealth through government expenditures for regional development purposes.

And at first it looked as though there was hope. But before long the things I've just described got watered down. Some of them didn't work. Others were just window-dressing. And soon the same types of people, if not the same people, were making the decisions. It was kind of a shuffling of chairs on the deck. I think Brian Mulroney saw the folly of the past ways and really did want to change, but my God, it's hard, even if you're prime minister, to change mindsets.

MICHAEL MACDONALD

ACOA was focused, not on pulp mills and big projects, but on entrepreneurial renewal and on small-business development. Back in the mid-1980s that was leading-edge thinking. In its design ACOA was excellent. However, almost a day after it was invented, Treasury Board officials in the Department of Finance in Ottawa started to pull back the control.

To them it was a very dangerous model. Here was an independent ministry outside Ottawa for the first time. If it turned out to be wildly successful, then the whole system would be in trouble. The agency, which was constantly accountable to Ottawa, ended up being audited all the time. When your projects are constantly audited and you're watched and monitored and your budget is cut back and you can't make commitments, you get gun-shy and that's what happened at ACOA. It stopped taking risks and only accepted projects it knew would be approved by Ottawa.

TOM MCMILLAN

I don't think anybody sat back and said, "OK, how are we going to screw the taxpayers to the wall?" But if we had sat down as a Cabinet and planned it, we could not have come up with a more brilliant way of achieving that end.

The program had its own momentum. There was no whistle blower. There was no one to sound the gong and say, "Does this make sense?" or "Where is it leading?" No one said, "Have the billions of dollars that we've already spent created the jobs and wealth that were contemplated? And if not, why are we continuing on this conveyor belt?" It just grew like ragweed; successive Cabinets just larded onto bloated bureaucracies to the point where every region in the country had its own bureaucracy for this purpose.

131

The history of DREE and DRIE and ACOA is really one of accumulating a steadily longer list of failed enterprises that ended up wasting millions and even billions of dollars of taxpayers' money because the programs were fundamentally flawed. They were based on the premise that bureaucrats and politicians could identify enterprises that had the potential to create wealth without government assistance. The truth is that those companies that received money and succeeded would have succeeded anyway, in which case the money was a windfall at the taxpayers' expense. And those companies or entrepreneurs that received money and didn't succeed couldn't have succeeded anyway, with or without government money.

DEANE CRABBE

A few years ago in Grand Falls, New Brunswick, the federal government invested somewhere between $15 million and $20 million in a pressed-wood pallet plant. This plant was supposed to produce pallets to be shipped down into the American markets. Now, anybody who knows anything about the forest land in the U.S. knows that they've got cheaper wood down there near the big markets. The wood would cost more here and the transportation costs would put us out of the market completely. But they spent the money and the mill operated about five or six weeks and then went flat.

TOM MCMILLAN

One of the classic examples that involved millions of dollars of taxpayers' money, both provincial and federal, was Benner Skis. The company was established in P.E.I. in the era of the Alex Campbell government, which really began the process of trying to force-feed these enterprises with federal and provincial government money.[2] Benner Skis was a branch plant of a German-based multinational company and was going to create a ski for the world market. Now you have to keep in mind that there aren't many hills or mountains in Prince Edward Island. The highest hill anywhere in the province would not qualify as a bunny slope at most self-respecting ski resorts in Quebec or Ontario. In other words, P.E.I. was not exactly an ideal candidate for an enterprise of this kind. But that didn't prevent the bureaucrats and the politicians from thinking it was a wonderful idea to build a manufacturing plant to create skis. Predictably the company fell flat on its face.

The main problem was that there was a built-in bias toward enterprises on which the government and the politicians could put up a great big plaque saying, "Built by the Government of Canada." This meant projects that involved building a plant were favoured over ones that didn't involve bricks and mortar. In P.E.I. there was lots of industrial space already, but the relevant grant went toward building a new plant and it didn't address some fundamental problems.

First, there were all kinds of companies around producing skis, and second, there was no domestic market. Very few people in Prince Edward Island were going to buy skis, let alone ski in the province, or in the Atlantic region for that matter. Moreover, the input costs were exorbitantly high to produce these skis. Electricity rates, for example, were twice the national average. Transportation costs were very high because the plant was on an island and the island was far from central markets. So it ended up costing more per unit to produce these skis than the company could sell them for. And of course there were all kinds of companies around, including the parent plant in Europe, that were producing skis of the same type more cheaply.

So after the federal government money and the provincial government money dried up, so did the plant and so did the skis.

ROBERT NIELSEN

A lot of ACOA money has gone to fly-by-night operators who set up some little business that was gone within a year, just as soon as the government money ran out.

DONALD SAVOIE

There have been a number of success stories, however. I was doing a piece of work on regional development in Newfoundland, and I talked to a fellow who told me that six years ago he had started with a small grant and he now had 90 employees doing a lot of high-tech stuff. He was making a profit and doing very well. And the McCains will tell you that they're in business because in 1956 they were able to get a $25,000 grant. We've had a few success stories that we should never lose sight of.

TOM MCMILLAN

There are some examples of companies and entrepreneurs that probably wouldn't have succeeded without help and did go on to create the jobs that were intended, but those are rare. If they were birds or animals, they'd be on the endangered species list.

When I first began, I guess like so many other naive and callow politicians, I thought we were going to do all sorts of wonderful things by approving grants to industries and entrepreneurs to help the unemployed and disadvantaged. But gradually, as I sat in Cabinet and on a board that approved all projects of this kind over $1 million , I started asking myself why on earth were we approving millions of dollars in grants to enterprises based in communities like Newmarket, Ontario, near Toronto, where the per capita income was among the highest in the world, let alone Canada!

This business of willy-nilly, from one end of the country to the other, doling out huge dollops of money that the federal government doesn't have, to create wealth and jobs that usually aren't created, should be abandoned, for the benefit of not only Atlantic Canadians, but Canadians across the country.

But if you take this support away, what will Atlantic Canadians do?

TOM MCMILLAN

Look, the federal government has been in this racket since 1969, and yet the disparity in income between Atlantic Canadians and other Canadians has not budged even 10 percent. The level of poverty and all the other indices that measure whether a program has succeeded or not demonstrate that the approach is a failure because it's inherently flawed. We have to distinguish between federal government direct grants to individual entrepreneurs and enterprises, and transfer payments that ensure that Atlantic Canadians have a standard of education and health and other services akin to those in the rest of the country. You can support transfer payments for that purpose without embracing this ludicrous notion that bureaucrats and politicians are positioned to pick entrepreneurs and enterprises that are going to be winners in the marketplace.

NOTES

1. The FLQ, or Front de Libération de Québec (1963–1970), was a terrorist organization intent on Quebec separation.
2. Alexander Campbell was the Liberal premier of P.E.I. from 1966 to 1978.

CHAPTER 17

DEPENDENCY:
ESCAPING FROM THE CARGO CULT

MILLER AYRE

PAUL BROWN

MURRAY COOLICAN

DEANE CRABBE

BRIAN CROWLEY

MICHAEL MACDONALD

TOM MCMILLAN

HARRY O'CONNELL

DONALD SAVOIE

A s we travelled through Atlantic Canada we kept encountering white elephants of every size — and in the oddest places, like strip malls and deserted fields. We began to understand the dilemma of people desperate to put dependency behind them, facing determined politicians eager to maintain the status quo. The unholy mixture of dreams, greed, vote-buying and short-term, unrealistic thinking had produced a long list of failed enterprises.

But ultimately this story was turning optimistic. We were encouraged by how many of the people we met were so positive about the future and clear about what had gone wrong. They knew who had been responsible and what had to be done to improve the situation.

— The Team

DEANE CRABBE

I like to compare our situation here in the Maritimes with the deer in the woods. They do quite well on their own if you leave them alone. But if you move into an area where deer yard every winter, and for three or four years in a row you cut down trees so they can feed on those plots, if you suddenly stop doing that, a lot of those deer will starve to death. I think it's the same way with help in dollars. If you get into the habit of receiving it, you become dependent on it.

MICHAEL MACDONALD

If you rely on somebody else for ideas, if you rely on them for direction, and if you rely on them for dollars and for continued support, you pay a phenomenal personal, cultural and moral price. If you're dependent, basically you have no future and you certainly don't have any sense of destiny.

PAUL BROWN

During and after the First World War the federal government decided that the Maritimes would be a source of raw materials, a sort of army outpost, and that the heart of industry, Ontario, was going to be in the heart of Canada. So we got the money and they got the jobs. It's kind of a Faustian bargain because that's not the way to build communities. It's the way to build dependency. As far as I'm concerned, transfer payments are pay bargains, pure and simple. The central part of Canada funnels money to the outlying parts of the country as payment for having the centre of economic activity in the centre. And I'm sure they feel very good about that.

DONALD SAVOIE

In the short term these grants make people feel good and optimistic, but in the long term very few of the businesses that get funding survive. When businesses fail, there's a feeling that outsiders came in and ripped us off. As a result, a certain kind of mental state takes over.

Is this what you call the cargo cult mentality?

DONALD SAVOIE

Yes. In the Second World War, the Americans built airstrips on some South Pacific islands and all sorts of cargo planes flew in and unloaded good stuff. The natives, who were hiding in the trees, had never seen a plane before and thought a silver bird had flown in and brought all kinds of things. You just cleaned a stretch of land, put some lights around it and a big silver bird would come. That's a cargo cult.

Now, the case could be made that in parts of this country we've had a cargo cult. We've put in the lights, sewers, water, industrial parks, streets and so on, thinking that we just have to sit back and watch the cargo come in. But it doesn't work like that. There are a lot of these parks in Atlantic Canada, Quebec and the rest of the country that are virtually empty. Not a sole occupant. You have beautiful industrial parks with lights, streets, water and sewage, but no activity at all.

TOM MCMILLAN

We've become hooked on short-term fixes and the idea that white knights from Europe or the States are going to come into our communities and overnight create successful companies. For a long time Atlantic Canadians thought that the answer to our economic problems resided with others who were going to come in and do wonderful things, if only we could convince Ottawa to loosen up the purse strings to help those saviours. We realize now that those saviours don't exist. A lot of the people who came in with federal government money to save us sold us the latest snake oil and ended up raping us economically.

PAUL BROWN

We've been told, and the media emphasizes it, that this is a disadvantaged part of Canada that doesn't have many prospects, and can survive only through generosity and handouts from the wealthier parts of the country that are more naturally given to economic development.

I think that's a crock. There's nothing standing between the Maritime provinces and development. We have to rediscover the confidence and the tradition of entrepreneurship that we once had and that made us famous around the world.

MICHAEL MACDONALD

The good side of the terrible pain our people are going to go through with the demise of a lot of these programs is that they are realizing that they are on their own and that nobody's going to save them if they are stupid, lazy or lack initiative. We're flipping back to a 19th-century tradition of tough, resilient Maritimers. You can't be a pussycat and live here and do well. You've got to be tough. The young people are beginning to realize that they're going to have to get out there and scratch and fight for themselves.

Maritimers are finally realizing that the government has become impotent and is not going to save them. There's a new, growing spirit of entrepreneurship in Atlantic Canada. The rate of new businesses and the participation by women and minorities in business are the indices that we use to measure the entrepreneurial health of a culture. A lot of people today have sole ownerships of small businesses, and some of them are grouping together in co-ops.

MURRAY COOLICAN

A lot of things happening in this region in terms of economic development and activity bear no relation to government subsidies or government economic strategies. People are simply taking the initiative and going out and doing things with what's around them and making things happen.

BRIAN CROWLEY

Let me give you a couple of concrete examples of the way innovation works.

A fellow I know makes Highland paraphernalia and bagpipe fittings. One day as he was reading the newspaper his eye just happened to fall on an advertisement calling for tenders from an aircraft company. It was looking for subcontractors to make airplane parts. He realized that with the equipment he had for making Highland paraphernalia, he could make the aircraft parts described in the ad. So he put in a tender and he won the contract. He now employs 12 people making aircraft parts, as well as maintaining his original bagpipe business.

Now, if you were in government, trying to identify people to whom you can give a grant to make aircraft parts, and you put an ad in the paper, this guy would never have applied because he wasn't an aircraft-parts maker. Because he stumbled across a bit of information that made him think of himself, his equipment and his workers in a new way, he was able to create new value for people and put new things into the economy that other people valued enough to pay for.

There's another example. The town of Springhill, Nova Scotia, up near the New Brunswick border, is what some might call a clapped-out coal-mining town.[1] One day in the middle of winter a man was out walking his dog. It was a snowy day, and he saw a little patch of ground where there was steam rising and the snow had melted. He went away, asked some questions and did a little digging. He discovered that water had been leaking into the old mineshaft under the town and had been heating geothermally. As a result, a whole new industrial park has now been built in Springhill exploiting that cheap energy source, which nobody knew existed until that man went out one day and walked his dog.

Now, if government is the agent of economic development, how could it know these things? It couldn't. It's only through innovation, through people putting together disparate bits of information and knowledge and coming up with something new, that economic value is created. You can't do that sitting around a table in Ottawa or in the ACOA head-quarters in Moncton. Only people on the ground know the time and the circumstances and understand the consumers and what they want. Indeed, even the people who come up with innovations often don't understand the nature of what they have discovered. When Coca-Cola was first put on the market it was marketed as a mouthwash. Consumers thought it was a lousy mouthwash but they liked to drink it. And it became the most successful consumer product in history.

The people who invented the motor car thought that the number of motor cars in the world would be limited forever by one factor — the number of members of the working class intelligent enough to be trained as chauffeurs. The inventors completely misunderstood what they had created. And government authorities everywhere tried to dis-courage the new industry.

When the automobile was introduced in North America, there were 20 million horses on the continent. There was huge demand for saddle makers, nail makers and blacksmiths, and hay was a major crop. All that has been swept away. It doesn't exist anymore. You can't go to a community college and become a blacksmith. You can, however, go to a community college and take courses in 100 different professions that did not exist before the automobile was invented. If we had allowed politicians to do what politicians do so well, which is to stop innova-tion because it threatens established interests, we would still be riding horses. We would still be making horseshoes and we would still be growing hay.

PAUL BROWN

Nova Scotians once set sail and piloted their ships around the world and had a thriving economy. I think we can set our sails again to capture the winds of the electronic revolution and find prosperity again.

HARRY O'CONNELL

On Prince Edward Island we have a one-million-acre farm, the richest soil east of Niagara Falls. If I was given that as a farm today, surely I could make a living out of it. Surely I could hire people who could also make a living out of it. There's no reason that a province with the acreage we have should be dependent on anybody. We should be able to pay our own way. And we have the ability to do that.

MILLER AYRE

Newfoundland is also well situated in terms of growing industries, if we can find the right ones. One of the real issues here is whether Hibernia will be the springboard for a new oil frontier.[2] Will it be another North Sea? I don't know. There is a good chance that Hibernia will be a legitimate frontier oil development and that Newfoundland will have the awful problem of dealing with prosperity instead of problems, of becoming a have province instead of a have-not. That would really be something. I hope we don't all move away before that happens.

Does free trade have anything to do with this positive outlook?

PAUL BROWN

If you listen to the Economic Council of Canada, free trade had the potential to produce 484 jobs in Nova Scotia. That was the anticipated benefit. I think it's much more profound than that. Free trade has shattered the foundation for the Canadian bargain that saw jobs concentrated in Ontario and money distributed to Atlantic Canada. Free trade makes it much more difficult for the federal government to use policy and monetary fiscal tools to sustain a bargain that has given us money but no development in our communities. It's levelled the playing field and changed the ball game.

MICHAEL MACDONALD

I was in government when the first free trade agreement was being negotiated. Although I had many reservations about the deal, I bought into it for the following reason.

In the Maritimes there are about two million people. With this agreement, overnight we gained a U.S. market of 50 million of the richest consumers in the world. For the first time we have an Ontario-style auto pact with New England. We have equal access to New England. If we can't build industries here and build markets there, we deserve to be poor. And that's why the entrepreneurial spirit of the new generation — their resilience, their cynicism about government and their disbelief in dependency — is a cause for hope. We're going back to Boston!

140

Now, to members of the Toronto elite, especially the literary and artistic elite, free trade is bad because they say that I'm losing my culture. Well, welcome to the heartland of English Canada. We haven't lost our culture and we never will lose our culture. What's happening is that Margaret Atwood is losing control of our culture.[3]

NOTES

1. "Clapped-out" is a Maritime expression meaning finished, depressed, not much left.
2. The $5.8-billion Hibernia offshore oil platform began operation in 1998.
3. Margaret Atwood was at the forefront of the movement, which included artists, writers, etc., to stop free trade because, as I understand it, they claimed that the agreement would cause us to lose our culture. We would just be absorbed by the Americans. Because the root of Maritime culture is closely linked to that of New England, Maritimers have a very different perspective of culture than the literati of "Uppity" Canada. Many Maritimers felt that, as usual, these landlocked central Canadians, and especially the Toronto "elite," were presuming to speak for all Canadians.

—————————— CHAPTER 18 ——————————

THE COMPASSIONATE "I"

JOHN CROSBIE
BILL MACKNESS
ROBERT NIELSEN
FILIP PALDA

Most of us on this trip were middle class, from various parts of the country and different ethnic backgrounds, but our families, broadly speaking, fit into that economic middle part of the population. We all enjoyed the advantages brought to us by our middle-class entitlements. These include baby bonuses, low university tuition, public transportation, health care, unemployment insurance, subsidies to film companies, art galleries, theatres, the CBC — the list goes on.

We took a hard look at the motivation behind these various benefits, many of which have been justified by the principle of universality. We came up with some very interesting answers.

— The Team

BILL MACKNESS

At all political levels in the country there is a major commitment to universal social programs. Middle-class entitlements, the social programs that the middle class believes it's entitled to, are a part of the universality arrangement.

If you don't think about it very much, universality has a nice ring to it. It is, however, very much an income-redistribution scheme that carries with it some quite untoward results, such as major subsidies from lower-income Canadians to middle- and upper-income Canadians. An image I use to illustrate middle-class entitlements is postal employees wearing out their shoe leather lugging baby bonus cheques around Forest Hill and other upper-class neighbourhoods where these cheques are obviously not required!

The university education system is a classic example of middle-class entitlements. That system draws almost exclusively from middle- and upper-income families, whereas the bulk of the tax funding comes from people at the lower end of the scale.

The individual who drives the bus to get the middle-class children to university in the morning is also contributing because he's paying a great whacking tax bill to underwrite the educational institution.

The political justification for universality is that it tends to co-opt opinion leaders in the middle classes: the media, the clergy, schoolteachers, university professors and so on. They get a wonderful deal, whereas the people down below them on the income scale are shipping money up to educate middle-class children. I think that these entitlement schemes have been a major bribe, if you like, to bring the middle class on side.

What we're engaged in now is damage control, but I don't think there's been any philosophical shifting away from universality.

FILIP PALDA

You're looking at one of the biggest beneficiaries of those entitlements. I have been feeding off government quite heavily most of my life and I think I'm what I'd call middle class.

My education has been almost entirely paid for by government. I did a Ph.D. at one of the best schools in the United States, paid for largely by the Canadian government. I don't know why they gave me all those scholarships. There was no reason for them to pay for that education. It's the kind of education that pays for itself. And the students most likely to go to university are students from families with incomes above the national average, those from the middle class.

JOHN CROSBIE

The only representatives of youth that politicians come across are those at university student organizations. By and large these students' viewpoints are quite narrow. You see, they're politicians as well, and they're not going to get re-elected to head up the student groups if they don't act on the basis that students should have more. The views they express are quite narrow and selfish.

FILIP PALDA

I take the train between Montreal and Toronto about once a week. Half of that price is paid for because the train is subsidized, so there's another few hundred dollars that I pick up along the way every year. If I became unemployed, I would pick up something like $735 a week for the length of my unemployment. The more income you make, the more UI you are entitled to. And this is a funny one. Unemployment insurance goes mostly to families whose income is above the national average.

Subsidies to the arts could be called middle-class entitlements: subsidies to all sorts of film companies, those festivals at Stratford and Niagara-on-the-Lake, the CBC. Ask yourself, who listens to the CBC? Any subsidies to the Canadian arts are largely consumed by people in the middle- to upper-income range. But subsidies to the arts are not a big hit on the budget.

But why are they called entitlements?

FILIP PALDA

When people get something for a long time, they start getting used to it and they start figuring it's theirs. When you build your life plan around something, you don't want government yanking it away all of a sudden.

Before a recent federal budget my mother was very concerned that the old age pension was going to be cut. She thought it was her entitlement even though she is from a middle-class family with an income slightly above the national average. But her plans were set years ago. She decided then to save less because she knew government would take care of her.

But weren't social programs established to help the poorest people in our society?

FILIP PALDA

You're right. Many of the programs that can be labelled as middle-class entitlements were created to help the poor. They were created to help people in trouble. The idea wasn't really to take the money away from the middle class and give it back to the middle class.

Americans target the poor a lot more precisely, but in Canada this notion of compassion has exploded. Now everyone's included. Everyone's entitled. It's a part of our caring way. But I would argue that this isn't caring at all. It is actually the opposite of caring. Compassion is a great excuse for extending these services, when everyone is claiming to be a victim and saying, "I'm entitled to this and that." We're compassionate, but we're compassionate in the wrong way and to the wrong people. Remember, it's easy to be compassionate when you're compassionate with somebody else's money.

BILL MACKNESS

When these programs were being brought forward I asked the obvious question, "Why not do away with universality and save an immense amount of money?" And a Liberal senator confided that the reason was, if you did that you wouldn't sustain the support of the middle class for the expansion of the program. If these programs had been restricted to the poor, I believe that the middle-class opinion makers would have been much less vocal in their support of the programs. When medicare came in, for example, there were any number of private or provincial plans working in the area of health care that had disaster-type arrangements connected with them and that left better-off people to look after themselves more.

But the social activists wanted these kinds of universal social programs shipped out to everyone. Since universal medicare came in, studies have indicated that the middle class and the richer populace consume a disproportionate amount of medical services, presumably because they are better informed and are more interested in looking after themselves.

FILIP PALDA

They've found that middle-class and upper-middle-class families tend to have better access to the Canadian health-care system because through their social connections they know doctors and people in the community who will get them to the front of the line.

BILL MACKNESS

So these people are actually getting more from the government than they are putting in and that has an important effect on the electoral process. That's why the middle-class opinion makers have such a disproportionate influence on public perceptions in these matters.

ROBERT NIELSEN

A few years ago the health minister said that New Brunswick medicare would no longer cover the so-called "snowbirds," the seniors who spend the winter months in the south, for more than three months. Previously they had been covered for six months. Well, this caused a great uproar. Letters to the paper said it was arbitrary and illegal. One asked when this abuse to seniors was going to end. It was as if the poor health minister was a cruel hawk about to swoop down and rob the poor snowbirds of their last savings.

Now, most of the snowbirds are among the better-off seniors. I wrote a column about it in which I said that this country treats us old people well, better than it can now afford. I pointed out that the over-65-year-olds consume 40 percent of the medicare bill. And here are these better-off people saying we should economize on somebody else. For a while I drew their wrath instead of the government, but in the end the government backed down, or at least put the issue on hold, which is just a way of burying it.

JOHN CROSBIE

One of the most difficult groups to deal with are senior citizens. You'd think they wouldn't be because by and large they're the most interested in politics. When you knock on the door during a campaign, a person over 40 is usually interested, whereas younger people couldn't care less. They just want to get you out of their face. But senior citizens as a group are tremendously selfish. You can't touch a thing that they now consider to be their entitlement.

In our first budget in 1985, Michael Wilson, who was minister of finance at the time, announced that we were going to do away with automatic cost-of-living increases in old age security (which might have amounted to a couple of dollars a month). Well, boy, the older citizens

146

went bonkers. A French-Canadian woman finally nailed Brian Mulroney outside the House of Commons and told him he'd had it. And the decision was reversed.

Supposedly the seniors have gone through the whole system and they understand the problems. But when it comes to their own share of the pie, they don't want it touched at all.

FILIP PALDA

I should feel pretty horrible about taking middle-class entitlements, but I don't. I just don't see the damage I've done to other people. It's an abstraction to me. I don't see that the programs I got were paid for with money forcibly taken away from others. So you might call it a degeneration of morals.

Would you give up your entitlements?

FILIP PALDA

I'd give up my entitlements if everyone else gave up their entitlements — the subsidized train rides, the arts, the CBC, education, health care and so on. I'll give them up if everyone else gives them up and once we give them up the taxes come down. You might also make me do it if you forced me to come face to face with the people who are paying for my entitlements, if I had to go up to them and say, "Excuse me, you're my designated taxpayer. I'm taking this amount of money from you, so fork it over."

BILL MACKNESS

I don't think that upper-income Canadians should take major subsidies from lower-income Canadians, which is the case with education and medical care. I think that there's strong political motivation for keeping this system in place because it keeps the opinion leaders on side.

I think that the medical-care system would work better with an element of price discrimination or price allocation within the system, and I expect that we will be driven there by demographics in the next decade.

One of the problems with our health-care system is, I guess, that two men and a boy could have designed it in the 1960s because there wasn't a problem then. We had the youngest population in the Western world, and running health-care systems for young, healthy populations is really easy. We're starting now to see the rubber hitting the highway because the demographics are running the other way.

PART FOUR

COUNTING THE BEANS

CHAPTER 19

HIDDEN DEBT

DAVID FRAME
MARK HALBERSTADT
JASON KENNEY
BRUCE LEGGE

LES LIVERSIDGE
PAUL McCROSSAN
DAVID SLATER

Unfunded liabilities are rather like endless bank overdrafts with no restrictions. When you add the amount of unfunded liabilities to the government debt, you come face to face with a total that is truly staggering: $1.75 trillion. How many zeros is that?

But many people, like the seven of us before we started this investigation, don't realize that these taxes on the future even exist. It now comes as no surprise to us that governments, provincial and federal alike, are not only secretive, but appear to be in denial about impending crises like those that were brewing during the time of our journey for what was then called the Workers' Compensation Board of Ontario and the Canada Pension Plan.

— The Team

The Workers' Compensation Board of Ontario[1]

BRUCE LEGGE

Originally the Workers' Compensation Board (WCB) was set up as an independent Ontario Crown corporation to ensure that it would be

free from politics and deal not only with the law but with equity —
the business of fairness. How can you pay a man for losing his sight,
or losing his leg, or breaking his back, or any of the dreadful things
that can happen in industry? You can never really do it, so you must
be scrupulously fair to give him as much by way of service and by way
of pension as you can. And that has been the doctrine of Workers'
Compensation since 1915, when the board was inaugurated in
Ontario.

LES LIVERSIDGE

The Ontario Workers' Compensation program has an obligation to
make sure that disabled workers are guaranteed the money they need as
a result of their disability for as long as they need it. That's only fair.

The board is supposed to have in the bank basically the same amount of
money that it expects it will need to pay for future worker benefits. The
shortfall, or the difference between what the WCB has in the bank and
its future payments, is the unfunded liability.

DAVID FRAME

The unfunded liability is the amount of money that hasn't been paid by
Ontario employers, but has been promised to workers in the form of
pensions to be paid for over the lifetime of those workers. There is about
$16 billion worth of commitments in the system right now [1994] and
only about $4.5 billion of funding.[2]

*How was the WCB run between 1965 and 1973, when you were
in charge?*

BRUCE LEGGE

The principle on which the board operated was that the money was
public money, employers' money, and existed for the good of the
injured workers. Therefore there was to be no waste and no debts. If
you have debts, you pay interest on the money you borrow, which
detracts from the money available to rehabilitate the workers. It was
that simple.

Because it is a public board, the WCB is controlled by the legislature of
Ontario. Legislation can change the benefits and the board then should
change the assessments, which are based on the risks in a particular trade.

So benefits are increased by legislation?

BRUCE LEGGE

They're changed by statute. When they're changed the board has to find enough money to pay for the change, so it increases the imposition on the employer.

What have been the major problems with the WCB?

MARK HALBERSTADT

It went from 1914 to 1980 without a debt. All of a sudden, from 1980 to 1994, it ran up a debt of close to $12 billion. There is something fundamentally wrong with the way things have been run there.

LES LIVERSIDGE

There's a lot of waste, mismanagement and overcompensation within the system.

DAVID FRAME

There isn't even a fundamental agreement on what the board is supposed to be. There are two essential views. One is that the WCB provides a social safety net and is a major part of government's social fabric. The other is that it's an insurance program.

The employer community is told, and we believe, that it's an insurance program, a mandatory insurance program. All the covered employers have to pay into that program. In return their employees' salaries are covered if they have a workplace-related accident, and the employers are protected from being sued by their employees.

But the government is saying that if this is an insurance system, it's not a government-backed insurance system. The stakeholders — labour and management and the board of directors — have a responsibility to decide how the system is going to be paid for, and the government doesn't have anything to do with these decisions. On the other hand, governments have been mandating all sorts of new costs from old accidents. Therefore part of our problem is that governments have been unwilling to define in legislation exactly what they are trying to do and what their approach is to workers' compensation.

BRUCE LEGGE

The government has to recognize that the WCB only administers the legislation that the government of the day provides to it. Politicians have to look very closely at Crown corporations that indirectly collect and spend money.

DAVID FRAME

The WCB is a huge bureaucracy and its responsibilities under the legislation are multifaceted. Since it is a much-criticized organization, a lot of people who work there feel they have to cover themselves. They're afraid to make decisions. They're often afraid to take a leadership role. The WCB is an embattled organization that doesn't like to make decisions and for the most part has to be forced to change.

MARK HALBERSTADT

My company has paid, over the past 18 years, more than $600,000 into the Workers' Compensation Board. The board has paid out a little over $200,000 to my employees. It has a positive $400,000 cash flow from my company. And now it's told us that the employers are responsible for many of the mismanagement problems that are going on at the board.

But we didn't start it. We did what the people at the WCB asked us to do. We gave them the money, and they've squandered it.

DAVID FRAME

What happened was that the government passed new laws that in fact almost doubled the cost of new pensions. Government has brought in most of the new costs. So while we can criticize the Workers' Compensation Board — and it does deserve some criticism — government has driven all the new costs and has said, "Over to you, Board. You've got to decide how to pay for them."

BRUCE LEGGE

I think that, without being judgmental, you can't promise more politically than you have the money to pay for — and that applies not only to a taxpayer who is given government services directly, but also to the indirectly funded and indirectly serviced organizations like the Workers' Compensation Board. Unless you provide the money, you cannot provide, by legislation, generous benefits, can you?

LES LIVERSIDGE

Political expediency bears a lot of responsibility for the current shape of the system. Workers' compensation became a political football. Legislative reform wasn't based on "Let's design the best, the most effective program," but on "Let's respond to some of the immediate political problems that we have." Opening up the purse strings caused a lot of people to receive overcompensation. That's the legacy we've inherited in Ontario.

And this legacy is hurting business in Ontario. I'm sure the government would love to say that it hasn't, but the people who are considering investing in the province are worried about it. If you cut the waste, mismanagement, unnecessary regulation and red tape out of the system, you would do a lot to promote business in Ontario.

BRUCE LEGGE

There are very few people who are as stingy with public money as I am because I'm the old school. You cannot have a lavish bureaucracy and save money. Every additional person that you give a signature to costs you money, costs your employers money. So you have to have a very tight-fisted administration with all social services.

The Canada Pension Plan

What was the original intention when the government set up the Canada Pension Plan?

DAVID SLATER

The Canada Pension Plan was always intended to be a partly funded and mainly pay-as-you-go plan. That is, the people who are getting the benefits now are being paid for by those who are younger and making the contributions.

Part of the problem is that the number of older people is increasing so much more rapidly than the number of people of working age. That means that outlays are growing much more rapidly than contributions. As a result, the actual funds in the plan will be exhausted rather soon. In addition, the amount of contributions people will have to make will be greatly increased. That's the problem with a deliberately unfunded pension plan.

When I say deliberately, I mean that the choice was made when the Canada and the Quebec pension plans were set up as to whether or not they would be funded — that is, whether the governments would collect enough revenues early in the plan to build up a big investment pot that could be used to meet benefits later on. Canada chose not to do that, but instead to fund each generation's benefits by the people who were still working.

So the intention was, in the main, to have the costs of each generation's pension requirements met out of the contributions of the generations coming along behind.

PAUL McCROSSAN

It's important to remember that the federal government did not have the power to bring in the Canada Pension Plan. To bring it in, Ottawa had to get the provinces to agree. The government proposed a contribution rate of 3.6 percent, 1.8 percent from the employee and 1.8 percent from the employer, which was far more than was needed to pay the benefits at that time. Lester Pearson's initial proposal was to charge taxes below 3.6 percent and raise the taxes as the money was needed.

Quebec said, "If you want our signature on the agreement, let's set a contribution rate that will be good for 20 years. Give us the money to invest and we'll sign on to bring in the national pension plan." So because the federal government had to obtain the provincial governments' consent, it set up this system of overcharging for 20 years and handing the excess over to the provinces. The excess money — the difference between the taxes collected (the 3.6 percent) and the money spent on pensions — was turned over to the provinces each year. And that's where the so-called CPP fund comes in.

All the provinces except Quebec spent the money. They said at the time that they were going to make lots of social investments, but the money basically went into infrastructure or was frittered away, depending on your political point of view.

Quebec decided that it wanted to re-industrialize. The province took the excess money and invested it in Quebec companies and in the stock market. As a result, the Quebec Pension Plan now has real assets. All of the other provinces just have notes saying we'll pay the money back in the future, but of course those so-called assets are just promises to tax in the future. They were handed the excess money each year from 1966 to 1986. They spent it and they signed IOUs. Those IOUs created the Canada Pension Plan assets.

If you go out today and buy a Canada Savings Bond, you think of it as an investment. What it really is, is a promise that the government will tax somebody to give you the money back in the future. The CPP fund consists of bonds issued by each of the provinces. But the money's been spent and what's been given back is a promise to tax.

Was there something wrong with the initial design of the CPP?

PAUL MCCROSSAN

The problem is that when the people in government planned the Canada Pension Plan and medicare, they were thinking in terms of the nuclear family: father working, mother staying at home, two or three kids. That was going to be the norm for society. They were thinking of the birth rates we had then. Given that sort of environment, the plan was reasonably well designed.

But of course it hasn't quite turned out that way. Starting in the mid-1960s the pill was introduced. Sexual mores changed. Birth rates dropped well below zero population growth. By the late 1970s it was apparent that we were headed for trouble. We had seen the birth rates fall right through to 1976, and we knew that if they stayed at 1976 levels we would be in trouble. And in fact they've continued to fall since then.

Didn't the Finance Department say, "Hey guys, there's a problem here"?

DAVID SLATER

Not just the Finance Department but the actuarial organizations in Canada, employer-benefit organizations, the Economic Council of Canada, the Ontario government and the Quebec government all said it.

Between 1978 and 1981 a series of studies of Canada's retirement-income system universally agreed that if we did nothing, then someday, sooner or later, there would have to be an increase in the contribution rates. What people didn't realize was how large the increase was going to have to be, or how soon it was going to have to take place. What clearly happened was that we did nothing. If the matter had been tackled earlier, we would have a less serious problem now.

PAUL MCCROSSAN

A national pension conference was held in 1981. The government wrote a report on the consensus arising out of the conference and proceeded to have parliamentary cross-country hearings. In Pierre Trudeau's last budget in 1984, he brought in proposals for changing the pension system. But then he resigned and John Turner was defeated almost immediately. So it was 1985 before the actual pension reform legislation came in.

DAVID SLATER

A lot of things were done to improve the system at that time, but they focused mainly on retirement pension programs, RRSP programs and things of that sort. For example, the federal government and all of the provinces greatly increased the portability of pension benefits, so if you worked for one employer and shifted over to another, there was a much improved possibility that you weren't going to lose your retirement benefits by changing jobs. A number of improvements of that sort were made.

Had we also initiated a modest increase in the contributions to the Canada Pension Plan and the Quebec Pension Plan, by now there would be a much bigger fund and the investment fund could be used to cushion the increases in costs that we've already seen. We didn't do that.

After all, the problems were not going to occur until the year 2000, or possibly 2010. In the meantime we had poor children, underfunded education, a road system that was deteriorating, the defence of the country, the problems of regional underdevelopment, high unemployment levels and the health-care system to worry about. There were lots of urgent problems around, so more pension reform never got to the top of the agenda. I guess people thought they could take care of it later.

What did the government intend should happen after 1986?

PAUL MCCROSSAN

When the original plan was set up, it was decided that the contributions would be fixed until 1986 and rise thereafter. They estimated the cost for the first 20 years, and that proved to be quite a good estimate. The cost in 1986 was just about exactly what was estimated in 1964.

How did this assessment compare with estimates for other programs?

PAUL MCCROSSAN

One of the things that I found out in 1979 was that the Canada Pension Plan was the only social program for which we had any estimates in the long run at all. The Old Age Security program had never been estimated for more than a year and a half in advance, as far as I could find out. The Guaranteed Income Supplement was never estimated until the late 1980s. The cost of medicare, to my knowledge, has never been estimated. We've brought in a lot of social programs figuring they were self-sustaining, but until 1986 nobody actually prepared the figures to determine if they could be afforded in the long run.

We had always gone along thinking that we could afford the programs. We were a wealthy country; we assumed we could afford these things and there was no real concern about the long-term cost — until we started to run into real economic difficulties after 1980.

How are the current problems facing the CPP going to affect my generation?

PAUL McCROSSAN

Let me put the problem in perspective. Let's look at people who retired, say, in 1975 after making CPP contributions for 10 years. My father's a good example. He paid 3.6 percent of his salary each year for 10 years, which was 36 percent of his salary over the 10 years. He received in return 25 percent of his final salary each year, indexed to the cost of living. And my mother continues to receive a survivor pension today.

Now, you don't have to be God's gift to the world to figure out that if you pay 36 percent in once and you get 25 percent out each year, that's a heck of a bargain. So the initial recipients, who were born around the First World War, got out, on average, about 15 times what they paid into it.

Now skip a generation. I'm a war baby, born in 1942. I will pay on average about five or six percent of my covered payroll over my 35-year working lifetime. The benefits I'll receive on retirement are worth about 13 to 13.5 percent of my covered payroll. So I'll pay almost one-third of what I receive.

Switch to my daughter, who's about your age. She finished university in 1995, so she's new to the workforce. She's going to pay 11.5 to 12 percent for something that's worth about 13 percent. The benefits will probably be scaled back, so she'll pay 11 or 12 percent for something that's worth 11 or 12 percent. So she gets no bargain out of this.

If you think of today's graduates, their grandparents got a great gift, their parents got a good gift. And they pay their own way.

DAVID SLATER

The young people in this country face benefits that are substantially less than I get and they pay substantially more for those benefits than I paid. It's a bit unfair to the younger generation, but how else are we going to fix the CPP?

JASON KENNEY

We're brewing a possible intergenerational war if we don't solve this problem fairly quickly. The baby-boom generation will be moving into retirement in a couple of decades, and the workforce simply won't be able to pay the benefits that were promised them. People of the younger generation, those moving into the workforce, will become increasingly aware of the growing burden. They will see pay-roll taxes for the Canada Pension Plan and the Quebec Pension Plan increase. They're going to see taxes generally increased to pay off the debt and we'll see them waking up to the fact that they've been robbed, that there's been intergenerational theft going on for two or three decades.

I think some political parties, in an attempt to appeal to the younger, working voters, will try to reduce the benefits of seniors' entitlements, and the people who benefit from those entitlements will try to protect them in the political forum. We're going to see a head-on crash of interests 10 or 15 years from now.

Most Canadians still expect to collect on all of these generous public sector pension plans. Many interest groups in the public sector keep telling their members that they have nothing to worry about and that these plans will be fully funded in the future. But there's not a lot of evidence that they will be.

Why are unfunded liabilities such a well-kept secret?

JASON KENNEY

Because they're invisible. Unfunded liabilities don't hit taxpayers today in the form of higher taxes or interest rates, as direct government borrowing does. Unfunded liabilities are future deficits. As any household knows, it's easy to delay problems until tomorrow. Politicians have the same temptation. They don't want to tell voters the bad news — that there are hundreds of billions of dollars in future deficits that we're going to have to deal with, one way or another.

160

NOTES

1. On January 1, 1998, the WCB of Ontario changed its name to the Workplace Safety and Insurance Board.
2. By 1997 the unfunded liability of the WCB had been reduced to $8 billion and by 2001 the WSIB had an unfunded liability of $6 billion.

CHAPTER 20 ---

DEBT DETECTIVES

DOUG DAVIS
BILL MACKNESS
WALTER SCHROEDER
DAVID SLATER

*A*s we came closer to understanding how the government actually conducts our business with our money, what had started
as an exciting trip across the country gradually turned into a serious and often sinister investigation. Who was responsible for this
massive debt? The answers were not easy to pin down. We learned
to be careful where we assigned blame and to avoid jumping to
conclusions because we were discovering that there was more than
one target.

— The Team

DAVID SLATER

As long as the visible part of the national debt was not too large, the invisible but growing part didn't seem to be such an urgent problem. Now that
the visible part of our debt is so large, and the invisible part arising out of
all of these unfunded liabilities is growing so much, the two together are
creating an urgency for action that didn't exist 10 years ago.[1]

WALTER SCHROEDER

Government just spent too much. The debt started small and just crept
up. Government had very small deficits in the period from 1965 to 1975,

but then we had a continuous round of more benefits and more expenditures, and since these small deficits weren't addressed, they just grew and grew because of interest costs.

The period we call the "Bad Years," when we really got into trouble, was roughly between 1975 and 1985. That's when debt levels accumulated so badly at the federal level. The Liberals, between 1975 and 1985, caused the problem, with their huge deficits. The three big budgets between 1982 and 1984 were the budgets that really broke the bank. Then between 1985 and 1995 nothing was done about it.

After 1985 the Conservatives just ran with what we called balanced expenditure budgets. In fact, in that time period all the Wilson budgets ran a surplus of about $13 billion. But it was interest of about $313 billion that killed Wilson and the Conservatives.

Is the debt primarily a result of government program overspending?

WALTER SCHROEDER

The program deficit — everything government does, expenditure and revenue, taxation and expenditure on welfare and everything else — has been relatively small over the past 30 years. It accounts for only about $40 billion of the total outstanding debt today. Let's put it this way: the visible government debt, as of March 31, 1995, was $546 billion, give or take a billion.[2] Of that total amount of debt, 90 percent was due to compounding interest.

We call compounding interest the silent killer because it creeps up on you. The first stage is a slight deficit on program expenditures, where expenditure exceeds revenue. What happens then is that the deficit has to be covered with borrowed money. And the borrowed money attracts interest.

Then the deficits continue and the interest continues and gradually you develop a situation where higher costs require more borrowing. More borrowing requires higher interest costs, which raise the deficit, and you get what we call a debt spiral. Gradually your problem is this interest factor, not the expenditure on program services. And that's the stage the government has been in for the past 15 years.

The feeling initially was that the deficit was just a small thing. In addition, economists kept saying that it didn't matter what the deficit was: it was the relative size of the deficit to the gross domestic product (GDP)

163

that was important. There was no need to worry if it was a low number. So politicians were just reacting to what some economists were saying. And as we all know, 18 economists have probably 34 opinions on 29 topics. The politicians could always find an economist who would support their position. So they didn't really care about the interest costs because the economists were telling them that deficits didn't matter.

And they forgot about the compounding interest.

BILL MACKNESS

My recollection is that in 1983 the federal debt outstanding was about 40 percent of the GDP. Ten years later we were up to about 80 percent of GDP. What we've done with this gradualist policy is simply to let the debt run so that it is now, quite literally, twice as large a problem as it used to be.

In 1985 when I went with Michael Wilson to the Department of Finance, the new government thought that putting expert individuals on a short-term secondment basis into minister's offices would be useful. I was the first, and I believe the last, such appointee. At that time there was a growing recognition that something of crisis proportions was brewing on the fiscal side and that something would have to be done about it. The spending was 54 percent in excess of revenues, and even a committed Keynesian would have to know that something had to give. I felt the situation was considerably more serious than it was generally perceived to be, particularly in Ottawa.

The deficit was roaring along at such a pace that I believed, short of some draconian movement to get the fiscal situation back into balance, what would happen was that the ongoing economic expansion would simply fund an inexorable rise in the debt load, which would then develop into an even worse crisis in the next business cycle. Which, I think, is a fair measure of what happened.

The bureaucrats, however, took a very soft line toward the fiscal problems. They were strong on rhetoric, but quite soft in terms of action. In its wisdom, the government chose to adopt that soft-line policy. Those offering advice were very capable people and well regarded, and their advice was politically attractive. Rather than suggesting some difficult spending cuts up front, the advisors said that the problem would go away if the government nibbled at the spending side over the next seven years. Their advice was actually quite well received by the politicians and in the business community too. The rhetoric was excellent, but the arithmetic was wrong.

Financial problems tend to get worse unless you deal with them up front and quite dramatically. What was happening was that the lack of will to cut spending caused the outstanding debt to continue to grow much faster than the economy that had to sustain and finance it. The predictable consequence was that five or seven years down the line there would be a much more serious problem. At that time, in 1985, the Conservative government's fiscal approach was very well received. I think that the government and the Cabinet believed the Finance Department's projections, which consistently said that the problem was manageable and would cure itself over time with some very modest restraint.

After nearly a decade of wishful thinking under the Liberals, the Conservatives followed the same basic formulations with a little more pro-business, pro-market rhetoric tossed in.

Then after more than a decade of these year-by-year budgets purporting that a gradual solution would work, we had a brand-new Liberal government, which immediately adopted the same basic stance. I guess the learning curve doesn't slope up quite as sharply as some people would like.

Why didn't the government use any surpluses to pay down the debt?

WALTER SCHROEDER

Perhaps I can explain this best by relating a story. We had breakfast with one of the premiers and congratulated him on obtaining a surplus. Later on, the bureaucrats who were with him said that they wished we hadn't mentioned the surplus to him. They said that one of their greatest problems with politicians was that once they knew they had a surplus, they wanted to spend the money. They said that what they, the bureaucrats, were doing was using the accounting convention to hide the surplus from the politician. By not letting him know about it, they were able to help contain the expenditure level of the greedy politician.

BILL MACKNESS

Once the debt gets large enough to control the situation, you have to run very large program surpluses, and politically that's not easy to do. The other alternative is that the bankers on Wall Street tell you that there will be no more money unless you do something to control the situation. I believe the latter alternative is driving the process. I don't believe that the fiscal reform in Canada today is a cerebral exercise. I think that it's on a script written by Wall Street.

The most visible sign of the mess we are in is our foreign indebtedness. In Canada since the Second World War, private sector savings have almost perfectly balanced private sector investment. On that basis there was no need to borrow any money abroad. We were saving enough as Canadians to finance all our commercial activity. Then when we began to run these massive government deficits, we began to dip every year into the savings pool in Canada and take a third to a half of Canadian savings and use them for current government spending.

The legitimate borrowers in the private sector who still needed the money were then driven abroad to borrow. We have an international debt now, in 1995, of about $375 billion, largely built up since the late 1960s.

This country had no need to borrow abroad. We're a very rich country. We borrowed abroad because we insisted on running government deficits, which cannibalized our savings and drove our legitimate borrowers abroad.

WALTER SCHROEDER

Unfortunately our debt is owed to foreign investors. Unlike Italy when it was faced with the need to borrow, Canada did not borrow domestically. We borrowed abroad. And today [1995], with a net foreign indebtedness of 26 percent of GDP, we're in a class all by ourselves. The next in line among the G7 countries is Italy at 11 percent of GDP, and it goes down from there. The United States is, I think, at 10 percent, and Germany and Japan have got more foreign assets than they've got liabilities. Even Belgium and Sweden, which are always cited in relation to Canada as having a lot of debt, are in good shape because they and just about every country in Europe owe their debt to their own citizens. But Canada has so much foreign indebtedness that if a foreigner doesn't lend us more money to pay the interest, we could default. So we have to keep the foreigners interested in Canada and assure them that we're credit worthy. Then they'll keep lending us money.

BILL MACKNESS

Foreign investors have been willing to keep lending us money only because we're a very wealthy country. We're politically very stable.

Certainly by international standards. So there is a high degree of confidence in Canada. If this were a more ragtag and poorer country, we wouldn't have gotten away with it.

To really ruin the balance sheet, you have to start with an excellent reputation. This also applies in corporate circumstances. Marginal corporations just can't put off the full financial disaster. A world-class developer, however, could probably get enough debt onboard to go down in flames. That's the ironic aspect of this. You really need a good reputation if you're going to ruin yourself financially.

What kind of financial shape are the provinces in?

WALTER SCHROEDER

We call the provinces a variation on the Clint Eastwood theme: the good, the bad and the ugly. The two good provinces are British Columbia and Alberta. The two ugly provinces, Quebec and Ontario, are in a league by themselves with massive deficits, even though we're in a pretty good economy. Then we have the six that are the bad middle provinces. The ironic thing about these six in the middle is that they've got the same problem the federal government has: their deficits are virtually equal to debt and interest that was put on the books before 1981 or 1982.[3]

The attitude of the provincial premiers, however, changed much sooner and more quickly than the federal government's, simply because the provinces are poorer. They didn't have the federal government's tax base or tax revenue capacity. So they cut back sooner, in about 1987 or 1988 — with the exception of Ontario.

Between 1985 and 1990 Ontario taxed and spent its way through a boom. And as soon as the recession hit, the simulations we ran showed that the deficit was going to explode. Because the economy was so strong then, not many people believed that there could be such a thing as a severe slowdown in Ontario, or that the way the province was raising benefits in the different programs could possibly cause expenditures to skyrocket to the levels it did. Social welfare, for example, in the 1988 to 1989 period was rising at about 14 percent a year. The question we were asking then was, "If welfare rises 14 percent in a boom, what will it do in a recession?" We got our answer very quickly, in 1991 and 1992. The government raised welfare benefits just before one of the worst recessions since the 1930s. The government couldn't have timed it worse. Welfare payments started to rise at 45 percent a year, so quickly that they surpassed education costs in Ontario! The benefits started to increase at the same time that the economy was dropping like a rock. Ontario is still recovering.

Shouldn't the financial community be taking some of the heat for our predicament?

DOUG DAVIS

The financial community is really to blame for what is going on here. If we think of the government as an alcoholic who is spending wildly, the investment community is the facilitator. It finances the debt on behalf of the government, and it does so willingly because it's collecting very large fees for doing so.

If the borrowing institutions, the governments, were corporations, they would be deemed bankrupt. They're insolvent. They can't meet their obligations.

We have a double standard here. We have a standard for the government, which is abetted by the investment community, and we have a standard for corporations and private industry, which is not aided by the system and the investment community. No one blames the financial community because it is a revered group. Its members are leaders in society and appear to be making a valid contribution. But government could not issue this debt without the financial community being there. You need the people who will sell the securities as well as the people who will buy them.

When someone calls me with a bond offering of a province or the federal government at a time when the government is not balancing its budget, I tell them that they're being unethical because they want me to buy for my clients the debt obligations of insolvent institutions. And I won't do that. I would much rather buy the debt of a nice corporation that is profitable and paying its way and whose assets aren't going to go away. I know then that my clients are going to get their money back.

The financial community collects big fees every time one of these debt issues goes into the market. And since the big brokerage firms are now owned by the big banks, the whole community is involved. The banks are not only sellers of the securities, they're buyers of them too.

Insurance companies are also there buying the debt, and so are the big pension funds.

Shouldn't the financial community warn investors about the dangers of extreme deficit financing?

WALTER SCHROEDER

The investment houses have a good relationship with the government. They sell government bonds. A few of them will speak out about the dangers of deficit financing, but generally it's not in their interest to raise any alarms.

DOUG DAVIS

The government has the power to control who is in the financing syndicates and what each member's share will be. These syndicates are financing groups put together by the investment community to share the risk and the rewards of government financings. If you are part of such a group, you gain rewards.

The government controls the selection of the members of the group. They also decide what percentage each member will have within the group. So if you're not in the club, you try to join, and if you are in the club, you try to increase your participation because the fees are virtually guaranteed once an issue comes out. So just to be in the syndicate is to produce a wonderful flow of cash by way of fees on these issues.

What's the difference between the rules for a private company that is attempting to attract investors and the rules for a government that is trying to do the same thing?

DOUG DAVIS

If a company is trying to find investors, legally it needs audited statements to prove that everything is aboveboard. If a company is not financially sound, that has to be recorded. If it's not recorded, the directors of the company are liable. In the case of government there is no statement. The government does something that corporations would never be allowed to do.

The double standard exists because the governments make the rules to suit themselves. The government is principally composed, at the parliamentary level, of people from the legal profession. Most of them have never studied Economics 101. As a result, they are making rules in an area they don't understand. If they understood it better, they might make better rules. Of course, since politicians want to be re-elected, they make the rules to suit their objective, which is to retain their popularity with the people.

Years ago when Darcy McKeough was the treasurer in Ontario, he met with financial analysts to talk about the province and how he was trying to get the budget into balance. I said, "Well, that's fine Mr. McKeough, but when do you intend to start repaying the debt that you've already built up?" And he said, "Probably never. Governments don't repay debt, they only borrow!"

Notes

1. According to the Fraser Institute, as of January 1, 1995, Canada's total debt, including unfunded liabilities, was $1.75 trillion.
2. As of March 31, 1999, the debt had risen to $597.7 billion. At the end of 2001 it stood at $549 billion.
3. By 2002 the financial situation in the provinces had changed. In surplus: Alberta, Saskatchewan, Manitoba, Ontario, Quebec, New Brunswick and the Northwest Territories. In deficit: British Columbia, Newfoundland, Nova Scotia, Prince Edward Island, Nunavut and Yukon Territory.

CHAPTER 21

BEATING THE SYSTEM

CHARLES ADAMS
JASON KENNEY
BARRY LACOMBE
STEVE MARSHALL

DAVID PERRY
ROD STAMLER
CATHERINE SWIFT

Canadians are carrying a tax burden that is higher than that of citizens in any other G7 country. Over the past 10 years Canadians have become increasingly frustrated and have started speaking out. The underground "cash economy" is thriving, tax-free, and the government seems powerless to put a stop to it. Tax rallies, like the one we visited in Pickering, Ontario, have been supplemented by budget-cut rallies, angry marches on the legislature and protests on Parliament Hill. People are angry and are speaking out, as they did at the rally we attended. But is anybody listening?

— The Team

Revolting Taxes

The following quotes are from people who attended the rally.

Janice Frampton, organizer of the Pickering tax rally
People are finally saying enough is enough. Forty-six cents out of every dollar you earn goes to support government. That's ludicrous. That's rape. That is fiscal rape!

Gary Hooper

I feel sorry for the younger generation coming up. They're something like $32,000 in debt the day that they're born. They don't have to smack a baby on the backside anymore to get it to breathe. All they do is whisper in its ear, "Your taxes are $32,000. You're in debt that deep!"

Brendan Catney

I've been frustrated for a long time now. I left a union job to start my own floral delivery business, and the last person I was worried about squeezing me out was my own government. I'm barely getting by now because the taxes keep going up and I can't make any more money to give them. I'm at the wall.

Sandra Lalor

I'm really pissed off. I am. I am fed up. Because you try to help yourself and they pull you right back down.

Rick Sergison

If you elect a majority government, you have elected a five-year dictatorship. Once you have King Brian, or King Jean, he rules. And because of party politics, nobody will vote against the leader. If they do, their political lives will be ended; they're out of there. So who are they sticking up for? The country, their constituents or their political backsides? The government spent $30 million to throw a birthday party for the flag. We've got people suffering and living on the street and we're spending $30 million to honour the flag? Well, the flag is red for one reason. It's blood and sweat; it's tears and red ink.

DAVID PERRY

A few years ago I didn't think that there was any possibility we'd have a real tax revolt. Now I think that the chances are that a tax revolt could take place in staid Canada. The tax level has increased dramatically, especially in relation to the United States, and people are beginning to feel it.

JASON KENNEY

We've reached a point of diminishing returns. Canadian families simply can't get ahead. Their disposable income shrinks year after year because the tax burden is going up and their incomes are frozen. We've seen the growth of two-income families largely because of this increased tax pressure. It is ironic, in a way, because I think much of the deterioration in family life is perhaps attributable to the economic pressures that people are facing.

It's a self-perpetuating cycle of dependency: people are forced into the workplace because of the tax burden, and because they've been forced into the workplace, they need help to take care of their kids. And while governments, politicians and interest groups come up with these grand schemes for tax-funded daycare, what they're in effect saying is, "We've forced hundreds of thousands of people into the workplace to pay for their increased taxes, and now we want to tax these people even more in order to help to take care of their kids in government-funded daycare centres."

CHARLES ADAMS

There's an iron law of history and that is, when people get mad about taxes, unlike other things, they're going to react. It may be violence, like a revolution or a rebellion. It may be tax fraud and evasion, or people may just pack up their bags and leave the country because patriotism is soluble in taxes!

Now, we know that taxes started the American Revolution, the French Revolution and the English Civil War. Rebellion upon rebellion throughout history was based on taxes.

The French Revolution is a great example because, although we know that they executed the king and the queen, most people don't know that they also took all the members of the tax bureau down to the guillotine and cut off their heads. One of the real problems that the Republic had, and later Napoleon too, was that there was nobody to run the tax system. They had all been executed. That shows you how mad people can get over taxes.

If there had been life insurance 300 years ago, I don't think the tax collector could have gotten coverage for any price. His was probably one of the most dangerous jobs in society. Many a taxman went out and never returned home.

The reaction against taxes has a long and predictable history. A hundred years ago in Canada, the Liberal finance minister said that the only way to justify tax was to use it to pay for the essentials of government; using taxes to pay for anything other than that was highway robbery. That philosophy doesn't fly today, but that's what the founders of this country believed.

All good tax systems tend to go bad when governments cannot control their spending appetites. Those who manage governments are spendo-holics, and whenever the power to spend and the power to tax are both in the same political body, the power to spend will always override the power to tax. The culprit is spending.

How do people react to increasing tax burdens?

CHARLES ADAMS

Many wealthy people have left the country because of the tax burden. Trying to soak the rich is an illusion. You can't soak them because they have the means to avoid taxes, and if they get mad enough, they leave the country. It's like a half-starved crow. He's not going to sit around and be shot at. When you tell the rich you're going to soak them, they pack up and go. But the aver-age person can't do that. He can't move to Lyford Key, the way E. P. Taylor did.

The only dependable source of taxation is the middle class. The middle class can't run and they can't hide. They have to put up with the tax sys-tem and they react in two other ways: with violence or by evading the system. When you see these signs within a society, it's a warning that something needs to be corrected. And governments usually miss the point. They think that correcting it requires cracking down on the defi-ant taxpayer. But when you have enough defiant taxpayers, it's a warn-ing that maybe the system is wrong and needs correcting.

Tax Havens

STEVE MARSHALL

Average people are starting to go to accountants, lawyers and tax plan-ners and asking questions that never occurred to them 10 years ago. It used to be that only large corporations or wealthy people could afford to get advice about structuring their affairs in a way that avoided taxa-tion in Canada. But now the average person wants to know about tax havens and how to utilize them. People are learning that there are options available within the complexity and ambiguity of the Income Tax Act and that there are ways to receive tax benefits.

I guess an accepted definition of a tax haven would be "a jurisdiction that charges little or no tax." The industry term is "offshore financial centre," which gets away from the negative connotation. The offshore financial cen-tres report tells you the various pros and cons of the different jurisdictions like Luxembourg, Jersey, Ireland, Cyprus, the Cook Islands, Grand Cayman and Barbados, which is an especially attractive jurisdiction for Canadians.

The Income Tax Act requires that individuals who are resident in Canada pay tax on their worldwide income. Corporations are also considered to be individuals for the purposes of the Income Tax Act. But when you go outside the country and create a corporation that is a separate entity for tax purposes, that corporation is not considered to be an individual residing in Canada. That corporation is outside the jurisdiction of Canada and is not taxable under the Canadian Income Tax Act.

For people whose business involves any sort of importing or exporting, the manufacture of goods outside of Canada, payment of royalties or commissions, consulting services outside the country and so on, it makes sense to look into a tax haven.

What the tax planning industry tries to do is help people structure their affairs in a way that avoids taxes legally. But some people evade taxes illegally using the very same sorts of structures, by not declaring income or not declaring their interest in certain corporations. Once they've started their tax haven corporation and once they've started the legal avoidance of some of the tax that would normally apply to their income, it's not too big a leap to cross the line between avoidance and evasion.

The line between avoidance and evasion seems to move all over the place and it has become the subject of a lot of litigation. And Revenue Canada, I think, is going to be looking at a lot of things that we traditionally thought were avoidance but now are being calling evasion. And if people weren't engaged in evasion, we wouldn't see the fiscal authorities out there with their badges and their pencils sharpened.

CHARLES ADAMS

Adam Smith in his writings on the wealth of nations said that tax evasion should not be a criminal offence. William Blackstone also believed that and wrote about it in his great commentaries on the laws of England. Montesquieu reflected on the same thing in his great book, *The Spirit of Laws*. He said that excessive taxation would inevitably result in extraordinary means of oppression, and when that happens, a country is ruined.[1]

Here we have three of the greatest thinkers of the Enlightenment all saying that tax evasion shouldn't be considered a crime. That's a crazy idea today, isn't it? But where there is suspicion and much waste in government, then the laws to protect the revenue will not be respected. That's human nature. You can't expect people to respect waste.

The Underground Economy

The following passages are excerpts from a conversation we had with an electrician named Matt. He explained to us why, like so many other Canadian workers, he has turned to the underground economy as a means of escaping an increasingly heavy tax burden. His last name has been withheld to protect his identity.

Matt, an electrician

Since I'm a licensed electrician, I have a trade and I can do things for people and they pay cash. Hundreds of electricians work under the table. Anybody with a skill or a trade — drywallers, plumbers, carpenters, as well as electricians — will usually work under the table for cash. Guys collecting unemployment insurance will work on the side too. Since they've got money coming in from the government, they can make more money that way than they can if they're actually working. I work under the table because I'm married and I have two kids and I have a mortgage and I pay daycare.

At the end of the week there's just not enough money from my job for anything else — not enough to go out for dinner or to buy my kids a toy. If I could bring home from my job what I should be earning, things would be fine. But after taxes and paying the bills, there's just nothing left over. The taxes just kill it.

I'm 28 years old. I've got to look out for my family's future. As far as the pension goes, I don't know if there'll be anything left for me by the time I reach pension age, so I try to put a few cents away whenever I can. But most of the money I make on the side goes right back into the economy. I don't have a big sock up in my closet where I'm hoarding all my money. It gets spent.

Are you worried about getting caught?

Matt

What can they do to me? Make me pay a little bit back? They don't know how much I've made or what I've done with it. It's not like I have an account somewhere down in the Cayman Islands. The money's going right back into the economy. I can't see them catching many people like me. If I was bringing home more money in my paycheque every week, I wouldn't be out doing this. I value my time at home more than I do just a buck.

CATHERINE SWIFT

The whole underground economy took off like a shot after the GST was introduced in 1990. Although the facts run contrary, governments keep thinking that they're going to be able to root these dollars out of the underground economy. I can understand the bureaucrats thinking this way because they can beef up their own numbers and justify their own existence by pretending they're the tax police. And boy, they're on a mission! But what ultimately happens is that the government spends $2 to collect $1 in the underground economy. The reality is that when government overtaxes people, and especially when people think that their tax dollars are wasted, they lose respect for government.

The people at Revenue Canada really think that they're going to chase down a few so-called offenders and this will get them great publicity and will result in tax compliance across the country.[2] This just shows how badly they understand the problem. The notion of going after some poor waitress who might be making $18,000 a year and getting $1,000 in tips that she's not declaring is just unfathomable. Not only is it not productive as a revenue-finding exercise, it's politically stupid.

What is Revenue Canada doing about the growth of the underground economy?

BARRY LACOMBE

In terms of enforcement, let me situate what we do. Work done by the department and by Statistics Canada indicated certain areas where non-compliance is a special problem and special initiatives were required. We've put together special audit teams to focus on these areas. We have to identify people who don't file and people who don't register for the GST. We have a very successful non-filer and non-registrant program. Through this program we have identified 509,000 individuals and corporations who have not filed their income tax. They're now paying their tax.

In addition, we've stepped up the publicity on prosecutions so that people will know that tax evasion is an offence. The consequence has been

177

a doubling of voluntary disclosures and a significant increase in the number of informant leads from taxpayers about tax evaders. I think the department has a very successful track record here. Ninety percent of the cases that we recommend to the Department of Justice result in successful prosecutions.

We've talked to people who don't think that Revenue Canada will ever catch up with them.

BARRY LACOMBE

Many people think that they won't get caught, but we're not dumb. We use network audit techniques which allow us to draw the relationship between someone's assets and the income needed to sustain those assets. People who say they won't get caught are using that income for something, and it will show up. There's a very high probability that these people will get caught.

ROD STAMLER

Our system of government depends on people complying with the law, people believing in the law and believing in government. We haven't got enough police officers or tax enforcers in this country to enforce all taxes, all the laws, all of the time, everywhere.

When people reach a point where they don't want to be subjected to laws and penalties, they simply rise up against them. They may break the law by getting things they want, like alcohol, which is highly taxed, or by hiring a plumber who doesn't charge GST. We saw it in Ontario when millions of people were buying contraband cigarettes because they were fed up with the high taxes.

CATHERINE SWIFT

But then, and this was the only instance I can think of in Canadian history, we saw a drastic decrease in underground activity because there was a major reduction in taxes on cigarettes.

ROD STAMLER

There's no question that whenever the public wants something illegal, a lot of profit can be made for those who are willing to break the law to supply those services. Some people, whether they're lawyers or accountants or whatever, are willing to compromise their ethical position in order to gather huge sums of money, and they are no different from the people who are actually involved in supplying a black market commodity.

And we've got to remember that one package of cigarettes doesn't seem like much, but when you've got millions and millions of people buying one package of cigarettes every day, a huge infrastructure evolves. In Canada the underground market grew to more than $1 billion. That can buy a lot of accountants, lawyers and other support staff to put in a system that launders money and brings shipments across the border.

How does the descent into the underground occur?

ROD STAMLER

Let's take the corner store, the ma-and-pa variety store that is selling legal cigarettes. Suddenly a store down the road begins selling contraband cigarettes for half the price, and all the customers start going down the street. Now that corner-store operator has to make a decision. If he wants to stay in business, he has to get in on the illegal trade of cigarettes. So he puts in a second inventory, a contraband inventory, and he stays in business. Now the flow from those sales has to be separated from all of his legal sales. Since he doesn't want it to show on his books and records, he'll think about opening an offshore bank account. So off he goes to a local money launderer. And this is the point where organized crime comes in.

Now along comes some other illegal commodity. It's not a very big step to move from illicit cigarettes to that other commodity. That offshore bank account is still in place and so is the money launderer. He can now move into a different world and might even slide some of his legal money into his offshore account because he's becoming more educated in illegal activity. And the more people who are doing this, the less likely it is that they will get caught.

Once given the opportunity for this kind of activity, organized crime can really grow and become a threat to our society. Once organized crime is in place it's very difficult to do away with it. If one activity dries up, as was the case with illicit cigarettes to some extent, the criminal organizations will get involved in something else, like smuggling cigarettes from province to province rather than from the U.S. into Canada, or smuggling firearms, weapons, drugs and alcohol. They were even bringing in frozen chickens from the southern U.S.

How would you describe the relationship between citizens and their government?

CHARLES ADAMS

When you get married you take a vow for better or worse, for richer or poorer, in sickness and in health. You tolerate a lot of things in a marriage, but there's one thing you don't tolerate and that is infidelity. I think that's true in our relationship with the government. There's a sense of infidelity when a government taxes you too much, when it takes too much of your earnings and your wealth and your enterprise. That's a breach of the contract between the people and the state.

We accept the government for its sins and its follies. But when it comes to taxation, we're getting into the area of infidelity. Governments don't make this distinction, and I think that they should.

There's a story in the old Taoist Chinese text.

> The Chinese emperor called in a sage and said to him, "I do not have enough money in the collection of taxes from the Chinese people. What can I do about it?"
>
> And the sage answered, "Follow the time-honoured tradition of taking 10 percent from the people."
>
> "But," the emperor replied, "I'm taking 20 percent and I'm still not getting enough."
>
> The sage explained, "If you get 10 percent, you will increase the prosperity of the people and they will pay more tax. A lower tax rewards people for their hard work. It rewards them for their incentive and their enterprise. The result is that wealth expands. The 10 percent will produce more wealth than 20 percent."

And this is what the ancient sage told the Chinese emperor 2,000 years ago.

NOTES

1. Adam Smith's book is called *An Inquiry into the Nature and Causes of the Wealth of Nations,* published in 1776. Montesquieu's *The Spirit of Laws* was published in 1748.
2. Revenue Canada is now called the Canada Customs and Revenue Agency.

CHAPTER 22

UNBECOMING CONDUCT

HANK JENSEN
MARCEL PELLETIER
ROD STAMLER

We'd always known that there was a certain amount of skull-duggery in all governments everywhere. We wanted to believe, however, that the majority of our politicians and bureaucrats possessed an integrity that was above reproach. In Ottawa we heard about the behaviour in recent years of some of our elected representatives and members of the civil service, behaviour that left something to be desired, to say the least.

— The Team

ROD STAMLER

One of the most difficult things for any law enforcement officer is to investigate a politician. The more powerful the politician, the more difficult it is. But personally I found the most difficult thing was that I had to report about investigations on a regular basis to the political level, to people who were perhaps entitled to know, but who had everything to lose if the investigation pointed to misconduct.

HANK JENSEN

The situation got out of hand following the McDonald Commission of Inquiry in 1981. It proposed that the commissioner of the RCMP should answer to the deputy solicitor general, who reported to the solicitor general, because the deputy would have more time to look into the activities of the RCMP.

ROD STAMLER

That was the turning point. It meant that before you could get a search warrant involving a politician, you had to report to the solicitor general, who might belong the same party or be a friend of the suspected person. Many solicitors general never interfered with the process and Prime Minister Trudeau never interfered.

Later, in the 1980s, there was a growing interest in what was going on. Not necessarily from the solicitor general, but from some of the executive assistants and political staff. This attention could undermine an entire investigation because in law enforcement it is important to be able to get a search warrant and to search, with justification and authority, offices or homes for books and records pertaining to a particular situation. But if the person in question is alerted, there's not going to be very much incriminating evidence lying around when the officers arrive with a search warrant.

Imagine I'm a new MP who has noble expectations about making a positive impact but zero experience. I arrive in Ottawa. How do I end up involved in some scam?

ROD STAMLER

First of all, let's assume that you're not heavily in debt as a result of your election campaign, and that you're an honest, honourable person who embarks on a mission to change things for the benefit of all Canadians. The problem is that you will get caught up in so much work on a day-to-day basis that you will delegate some of your power to your subordinates. You believe that these people are acting as honestly and aboveboard as you are, but they may not be. You may be drawn in by a fellow politician. Let's say the executive assistant to a powerful minister asks for your assistance. You may become involved, unwittingly perhaps, and soon you're supporting an improper activity.

Even if politicians are well intentioned, the system might somehow use them because they're the ideal people to hide behind. They're honourable members of Parliament who would never do anything wrong. Eventually they could become corrupted.

When I was the director of commercial and economic crimes, I was responsible for investigating government wrongdoing with respect to public funds. I gained insight into the sorts of activities that occur when public servants or departments get a lot of money to spend, or when a politician wants to be re-elected in a particular riding and wants to build some kind of facility there at the taxpayers' expense. Once the facility or program is approved, many people want to get to that trough to pick up some of the money that's flowing through it. They know the politician is getting a benefit and they know that perhaps some public servants were improperly involved in setting up the activity.

The breakdown starts from the top, with the politician saying, "I want a facility built in my riding." Then there can be a decay in the attitude of public servants with respect to the spending of public money. Among major corporations, the ones that are most susceptible to fraudulent activities are those in which there is some corrupt activity happening at the top.

When I started in 1970 I was told that spending in the federal government had gotten out of control, and in the next four or five years I realized that a large number of government officials were either condoning or participating in activities that involved things like kickbacks, contracts that were totally unreasonable and so on. And this extended right up to the ministerial level.

Now, I must say that quite a number of politicians were not, and are not, corrupt. They are upstanding individuals.

But aren't they all supposed to be upstanding individuals?

ROD STAMLER

They're all supposed to be, but they're not.

HANK JENSEN

Many businesses make donations to political parties that they would rather not make. But what are they going to do if, in order to get a government contract, a demand is being placed upon them to pay a portion of the proceeds of that contract to someone, or to a particular political party? There is so much potential for abuse that an insider with the appropriate connections has a much greater opportunity than a normal competitor who does not have those connections.

ROD STAMLER

I certainly saw a number of cases where this kind of activity occurred. Many contracts, of course, were granted honestly, honourably and aboveboard, but a number of contracts fell into that questionable area.

HANK JENSEN

There were an overwhelming number of investigations in the 1970s and 1980s.

After I left, there was a measure introduced that would severely limit and restrict the ability of the RCMP to conduct any investigation of any member of Parliament.

Marcel Pelletier's Story

MARCEL PELLETIER

In 1983 I was appointed law clerk and parliamentary counsel of the House; basically I was the legal counsel to the House of Commons.

If the RCMP showed up at the House with a warrant to search some offices because they had reason to believe that some criminal act had taken place, my job was to look at the warrant and make sure that it was prepared properly in accordance to law — that it was issued by the proper authorities and so on. If the documents were in order, I had to advise the Speaker accordingly.

The Speaker, who makes the decisions on behalf of the House, would look at the document and determine whether it was proper to allow the search to take place. Most of the time the Speaker didn't prevent the police from doing their job because normally the documentation was in order. The Speaker couldn't prevent the officers from doing their work just because it might give the House a bad reputation. Neither the Speaker nor the House can be perceived as preventing the normal course of justice from taking place.

For many years these calls from the RCMP were very rare, but in the 1980s there was a major increase. Usually these police visits were the result of allegations that members of the House had misused the discretionary funds given to them for the administration of their constituency offices. These discretionary budgets for members are relatively recent, and for some they offered an opportunity to do things improperly.

There is a board within the House of Commons called the Board of Internal Economy of the House, which is essentially an administrative body created by law to oversee fiscal administration for discretionary budgets of members of the House. In 1990 there was a proposal to amend the Parliament of Canada Act, Bill C-79. The proposal gave this board the power and authority to proceed with its own investigations. Whenever an allegation or a complaint was made, the Board of Internal Economy could stop the police investigation and proceed with its own. And while the board was conducting its own investigation, the police had to put a freeze on its investigation and wait for the board's results. It was like telling the thief that the police were two blocks away.

The Board of Internal Economy is made up of MPs representing both sides of the House. It is chaired by the Speaker of the House. The Deputy Speaker is also a member. There are two Cabinet ministers, the leader of the official Opposition or his representative, and private members from both sides. I objected to this process because it created a special regime for members of the House of Commons, a regime that is not available to you and me as private citizens. If I commit a criminal act, if I defraud someone, the police are going to be on my doorstep very shortly and I will be arrested as provided for in the Criminal Code. The Criminal Code applies to everyone equally in this country — or it should.

I thought this amendment to the act was interfering with the principle that everyone is equal under the law, particularly criminal law. There shouldn't be a refuge or a shelter for parliamentarians by the mere fact that they are parliamentarians. If they commit some criminal activity or wrongdoing, they should be submitted to the same regulations, the same laws, as any other private citizen.

Most members of Parliament go on doing their business without breaching the law. Why should this provision in the act protect the wrongdoers? It wasn't right.

I was called before the committee that looked at Bill C-79 as an expert witness, and I told them my view. The members disagreed with me and said that I didn't know anything about the political process. They were the politicians and it was up to them to decide what was proper and what was not.

Several months after all of the meetings I was called to the office of the clerk of the House and was told that my services were no longer required. I was a free agent and I was law clerk of the House of Commons no longer. So in clear language I was fired.

I knew a lot of people on the Hill who shared my view but it was extremely difficult for them to come out and say anything. Considering what had happened to me, nobody wanted to risk the same consequences.

I'm quite happy today and life is beautiful. But I think the moral standards on the Hill are just the same.

CHAPTER 23

ACCOUNTS, ACCOUNTING AND ACCOUNTABILITY

CHARLES ADAMS
PAUL DICK
KEN DYE
MAX HENDERSON
ALAN ROSS
WALTER SCHROEDER

By this time we were thinking that we were well informed on the ways of government. We now knew that the responsibility for many of the country's problems lay scattered and often hidden in a variety of places and among a great number of people.

We had assumed, though, that the members of this huge corporation called "government" knew how to keep track of our money, even if they didn't know how to spend it wisely.

But no ... even in Bookkeeping 101 they had failed.

— The Team

CHARLES ADAMS

We might all do well to remember the rabble of Rome. There was free bread for the rabble of Rome. There was free entertainment in the Coliseum with lions and gladiators for the rabble of Rome. The rabble of Rome got all of these handouts from the government. Ultimately they had a welfare state and it broke Rome!

You can't spend money you don't have. No, that isn't true. Government can spend money it doesn't have because it can push the debt off on our great-grandchildren and they can pick up the tab. All we have to do is pay the interest. We've discovered a clever way of borrowing money that we don't have to repay. We can just roll it over, and when we die our kids can pick up the tab.

And of course that's outrageously immoral. We should pay for our own goods and services. We have no right to push this off on somebody else. We should pass on to our kids a full treasury, not an empty one. We should pass on to them a debt-free society, not a society burdened with debt.

If we were at war, it might be different. If we had to protect ourselves from a foreign invader, we would have a right to go into debt and let them pick up the tab because we'd be passing on to them a country free of foreign domination. But other than that, we don't have this right. There's a moral issue here that we've lost sight of.

ALAN ROSS

There's no question that the ethics of government, the integrity of government, have changed. I guess it's a mirror of our society. When you hear that when they were preparing a budget, the people in the Department of Finance used the most advantageous estimates in their interest rates, or their foreign exchange, or their unemployment figures, you have to conclude that they lied. That's a morality issue.

PAUL DICK

The politicians have to take some of the blame because they aren't demanding that public servants be accountable to them for putting the Estimates together. But public servants must share the blame because they're the ones who love the system. In fact, everybody must take a share of the blame because nobody is demanding accountability.

Nobody has insisted on better programs. The politicians haven't, the people of Canada haven't, the press hasn't. There have been people who have tried to get more accountability into government but the bureaucrats have pushed them out, fired them or retired them because the bureaucrats don't want the system changed. If the system stays cloudy and murky, then they have no accountability. They're accountable to no one, and they just carry on. Not all of them, though. I know some public servants who are really frustrated, who are seriously dedicated and would like to have more accountability, but their voices get lost.

ALAN ROSS

A number of people were concerned. The auditor general in 1976, Jim Macdonell, blew the whistle. He did it in a way that was politically embarrassing and generated a lot of discussion. We even had a royal commission on accountability. But it was partly a cosmetic response by government and it eventually emasculated the auditor general's position.

The government created the office of comptroller general who was to be the most senior bureaucrat at the deputy minister level.[1] But in fact the comptroller general had no mandate to do anything. The government never gave this senior financial advisor the powers that Mr. Macdonell had intended to ensure visibility and accountability.

KEN DYE

The office of comptroller general has been merged into the Treasury Board, so the role has been diminished considerably from what MacDonell envisioned.

How do our leaders generally react to the auditor general's report?

ALAN ROSS

The major sin in government is to embarrass the government or a minister. The government spends a lot of time putting the correct slant on problems or managing embarrassing situations. The auditor general's report is now extremely well managed. People in government know the public can absorb only so many major headlines a week, and they make sure the auditor general has his headlines for two days, and then some other major announcement will be made.

KEN DYE

The media aspect of the auditor general's job started with Max Henderson and continued through Macdonell's and my time. There's a lockup and quite a fanfare, and then the report dominates the papers for one or two days.[2] If you issue a report on Tuesday, it's big news on Wednesday and you get some thoughtful articles on the weekend, but then it's gone. Something else overtakes it — a fire in a local community or some scandal.

Someone told us that you were the most unpopular auditor general in the history of Canada.

MAX HENDERSON

I was unpopular because I exposed so much of their waste and extravagance over the years, and I got such tremendous press for doing it, that in no time at all I became a folk hero. And that put me in competition with the politicians who liked the media. Mr. Diefenbaker and Mr. Pearson accepted it for what it was, but Mr. Trudeau decided he had to do something about it because I was giving severe competition to his ministers. A series of events followed that made my life difficult: downsizing the salaries of my men, freezing my staff and trying to prevent me from disclosing so much in my reports.

I suppose I took a risk, but I didn't give a damn. I had come from business. I was a professional man. There was a job to be done, and I went to work and did it.

When Trudeau introduced a bill in the House of Commons to cut me down to size, there was such an uproar across Canada that he withdrew it, on December 3, 1970. I went right after him for the rest of my time, until I retired.

I hate to brag, but I prophesied what was going to happen: the depreciated dollar, the incredible size of the national debt, the terrifically high taxes that would sap the incentive of our people. I warned them. I showed them that the staffs were multiplying, mushrooming, blossoming out. Expenditure had gone up 500 percent from the time I started.

A lot of people don't think too much about this kind of thing until they're woken up. I worked on the basis that I had a job to do. I didn't give a damn what the outcome was. I knew I was there until I was 65. They couldn't get rid of me — that's one of the advantages of the job. As I told Ken Dye, and as I told the present auditor general, "You've got to get in there. Don't pussyfoot it. Hit them with a two-by-four." That's the only thing they understand, these politicians.

If the auditor general is disliked or controversial, good for him. That's what he should be. Then he's doing his job. The first fellow raised hell back in 1878. He was so distrustful of the government in those days that he kept the spare cash in a box, and if politicians wanted to travel they had to ask him for the money. He was both the treasurer and the auditor general!

KEN DYE

The politicians of the early 1980s who might have done something with respect to the deficit and the debt would have reacted more vigorously if the people back in their constituencies had been more riled up. We produced documents for Parliament that explained carefully what the deficit was. People used to mix up deficit and debt. They wouldn't know the difference between an annual deficit and an accumulated deficit. When you start using bean-counter terms, people don't understand them. I wanted to make sure that parliamentarians understood the numbers. I even drew pictures for them. In the 1984 report I used expressions like "Mortgaging the country to buy the groceries." You'd have thought somebody would have listened then.

But then, the auditor general's job is not to control spending. That's Parliament's job. That's why we elect members of Parliament.

Is the government's accounting system in good shape?

KEN DYE

The government doesn't cost its programs the way a company does. It doesn't have a costing system. It really is just a cash-receipts and cash-disbursement system dressed up to look like a full accrual system. It is like going from just operating a bank account to recognizing that you've got liabilities. You may have bought something, but haven't paid for it, or you've got inventories around, or you've got people to whom you owe money, but none of this has hit the bank yet. To know what's going on you have to go from an accounting system that records just bank transactions to one that reflects the full economic reality.

PAUL DICK

The way the government does its accounting doesn't make sense to the average person. As a matter of fact, the Estimates today are in a form that 99.9 percent of the people in this country haven't a clue how to read. It's a third language: it's not French, it's not English. It's accounting, but nobody understands it. You at least understand the statements of Bell Canada or Alcan or one of the banks, but nobody except bureaucrats understands the public accounts and the Estimates procedures.

I asked the managing partners of each of the six major accounting firms in the Ottawa area to sit on a committee for something I was trying to develop, and five out of six said that they could not understand the government's accounting systems or the government books. They could not read them. And the one that did admit that he could understand them had worked in government for 10 years. If they didn't understand, I don't know who does.

Quite frankly, the government's accounting system would be considered illegal if it was used by a corporation. No company would be allowed to deliver statements in the private sector the way the government does. It would be out of business!

Accounting's a kind of dry subject to try and make sexy, but it runs every company and every organization. They all have to do a little balance sheet and an income statement and show where their expenditures are. But I've never seen an income and expenditures statement from the Government of Canada. I've never seen a balance sheet in the Government of Canada. There aren't any.

ALAN ROSS

It would be very difficult for the average person to understand the cost of government by looking at the Estimates or the public accounts. If you were to ask the cost of the Indian program or the Old Age Security program, or the young offenders program, you would have a very difficult time trying to understand what those costs were, and you'd have an even more difficult time finding out what anybody was going to do about it. But has anybody asked to see the financial operations of the Department of Health or the Department of National Defence? If nobody asks the questions, then who cares?

WALTER SCHROEDER

To really understand what government does requires accounting and economic skills, and it requires time. Most people couldn't care less. They just worry about their present tax situation and leave it at that.

MAX HENDERSON

Canadians aren't given to rallying very much you know. We're an apathetic lot. When Jean Kirkpatrick was the American ambassador to the United Nations, I asked her one day what she thought of Canadians. And she said, "My dear friend, they're like vichyssoise. Stiff and hard to stir."

192

NOTES

1. The Office of the Comptroller General was merged into the Treasury Board in 1969. Today's comptroller general has little of the importance or influence that the original position held.
2. When reporters are given an early look at a government document, such as a budget, they are not permitted to leave a lockup area to file their stories until the content of the document has been announced to the Commons and the public.

CHAPTER 24

THE FOLKS
IN THE HOUSE ON THE HILL

JOHN CROSBIE
PAUL DICK
MONIQUE LANDRY
TOM MCMILLAN
DONALD SAVOIE

Walking through the Parliament buildings on a Saturday evening, our footsteps in the corridors, we were all curiously quiet. Although many of us had been here before, on school trips and family vacations, we felt we were encountering an older, more refined period of history in these amazing, cathedral-like hallways. The reality of our recent, often disappointing and worrisome discoveries, many of which we knew originated here, clashed with a more romantic, unsullied vision of our country's glorious past. Later we all admitted to a sort of uneasiness about being there, as though knowing what we did, we were there under false pretences, about to betray something sacred.

When we walked into the House of Commons it was empty, of course: green velvet seats, polished wood and brass, stained-glass windows through which the setting sun was throwing its last rays. There was absolute silence. No sign at all that this was a battleground. No screaming echoes of the rude, insulting televised scrambling of Question Period. It was peaceful. It was inspiring. And it was full of ghosts.

We sat in some of the politicians' places — the prime minister's, the leader of the Opposition's, some backbenchers' — looking for clues to their personalities, their existence even. Did we hope to find ancient names carved into the desks? Probably.

It was an irony not lost on us that we had finally arrived at the place where the real answers to our questions could be found — here in Parliament, where we send honourable men and women to represent us and give them the power to speak and act on our behalf — but the House was empty. No one except an extremely pleasant and helpful security guard was there to answer our questions.

— The Team

JOHN CROSBIE

The House of Commons today is a TV adjunct. The only thing that counts is Question Period. The opposition parties spend all morning thinking up questions to embarrass the government. And the government politicians spend all morning thinking up answers to possible questions and wondering how they can put down the other side. This show goes on every afternoon in Question Period, and that's all that Parliament amounts to anymore.

PAUL DICK

Parliament hasn't changed as much as politics and the attitude toward politicians have changed. Politics was once considered a noble profession, but today it's not thought of too highly.

JOHN CROSBIE

Our Parliament is very frustrating for the members because they are by and large, ineffectual. But as an MP, I wouldn't go home to my district and say, "Look, I'm ineffectual, but I'm the best ineffectual candidate you could send up, so vote for me."

Ordinary members of Parliament — that is, government members who are not in the Cabinet, or opposition members — are pretty well powerless and have very little influence. They can still do a job for their constituents — straightening out this man's unemployment insurance problem or this woman's rent problem — but they don't have much influence in the party or on policy, and they're a very frustrated group.

195

PAUL DICK

Members of Parliament have to adhere to party discipline and follow the leads of the whip. The Canadian system is slowly maturing but it hasn't matured into the flexible system that the Parliament is in London.

In Canada when the government introduces a bill, it expects the Senate to pass it. If the Senate ever stops a government bill, it becomes front-page news. In England the House of Lords frequently doesn't pass government bills. In parliaments outside Canada, government bills are often not passed by the other house. Here it's supposed to be a rubber stamp.

If a politician doesn't follow the party line, the press will start saying that the party is split, and that puts extra pressure on the politician to follow the party position. There's very little breaking of party ranks when it comes to a vote. In England and Australia and other countries, however, breaking party lines in votes is not infrequent. Here the Cabinet and the prime minister have a greater degree of control than in most democratic institutions.

JOHN CROSBIE

The prime minister is becoming more like a president. It's really quite humorous to see how it operates. The prime minister has a staff whose job it is to make sure that he can't get blamed for anything. If anything bad happens, it's the fault of one of those turkeys in the Cabinet. They now regard the leader as sacrosanct. He's not the first among equals anymore. The prime minister is the supreme being and the Cabinet ministers are peasants down below and lucky to survive.

What motivates our MPs?

DONALD SAVOIE

Politicians are motivated by winning and getting support. Their sole motive is to win and to do good. And if they can't win, they can't do good. No sense being pious about this fact. MPs will tell you, "If we can't win, we can't stay here and do good." In order to win, you have to spend.

An MP will say, "Give me this one thing, this industrial park, this small-craft harbour. Give me this project and I will win. My people, my riding executive, my chamber of commerce, they're all after me. Give it to me. If you give it to me, I'll win. You'll have my seat." That's a pretty powerful argument.

TOM MCMILLAN

It is believed that some significant political advantage accrues to the politicians who are photographed in their local newspapers cutting ribbons. I can honestly say, though, as a politician who was in Parliament for 10 years, that the political advantages that politicians attach to these kinds of activities are greatly overestimated.

DONALD SAVOIE

Elections are won or lost because of broad policy areas like free trade. Rarely will they be lost because you didn't bring in a small-craft harbour. But don't try to convince an MP who goes home every weekend and spends Friday, Saturday, Sunday and Monday in his or her riding that local projects are not part of the game. Because he or she faces pressure every weekend for the small-craft harbour, or for that industrial park, or whatever.

JOHN CROSBIE

The real issues today in Canada do not get discussed at election time because the politicians are convinced that the public will not accept any tough measures or any tightening up. If you say to the public, "Look, vote for me. We've got a financial problem so I'm going to have to cut back, and we're going to have to stop this lavish spending on the social security system," the public will vote against you. They will simply not support you if you go to them on that basis. That's the dilemma. The real issues today in Canada do not get discussed at election time. Politicians are convinced they should not discuss any serious issue during an election.

DONALD SAVOIE

When you talk about spending, principles belong in the Department of Finance. They don't belong with MPs and ministers. That's not part of the game.

MONIQUE LANDRY

And when a government comes to power it doesn't just cancel what the others have put into place; it adds on to it. For years and years we've been adding programs to try to keep our electorate and to make sure they would elect us next time. I think that's a problem.

When you're in Cabinet the political life doesn't give you time to look deeply into government operations. You're a member of Parliament, you're a Cabinet minister, you've got your own department. You've got the House, Question Period and all the meetings. You don't have time to go deeply into all government programs. So you make your judgment based on what other ministers bring to Cabinet.

DONALD SAVOIE

If you're the new MP from Kicking Horse Pass, you come to Ottawa with good intentions, and you decide that your role will be to bring things to your riding and your community and to do whatever you can to act as an advocate on behalf of your riding. MPs over the years have viewed that as a noble role.

But when you talk about deficit and debt you hear, "Well, that has to be resolved at the national level. Don't look at me. I'm just a little MP. I go to Ottawa. I don't know how the big town works. There's bureaucracy. There's Cabinet. There are ministers. I haven't got a clue. What I'm here for is to speak on behalf of my region and I'm gonna do that and I'm gonna knock on whoever's door I need to get things done down here."

That's what motivates MPs. And in fairness, our system is built around that. No one takes a course to become a politician. It's like motherhood. They're supposed to know how it works immediately. So new MPs arrive in this town with its big bureaucracy and complex system and they get lost. It takes years to understand Ottawa and to be able to know how it works. Going into caucus and talking about a budget that's two billion bucks? MPs can't get their heads around that. They can get their heads around something that's in the headline that morning in *The Globe and Mail*, but not program spending or a debate about what should and should not be cut.

Most MPs don't have the knowledge. They don't have the capacity. They don't have the ability. They get a briefing and the minister of finance will stand up in caucus and say, "Here's what I'm thinking of doing on the tax side, on the spending," but there's no time, or capacity, or willingness to get into details of those decisions.

TOM MCMILLAN

Vision for a politician is the next election. Eternity is the election after that. And beyond such a scope, I don't think politicians have the capacity to give much thought to decisions that are being made.

In the future I don't think the leadership is going to come from the politicians. Nor will it come from the bureaucrats. I think it will come from the public. There has to be widespread recognition from one end of the country to the other that the federal government is costing much more than it ought to cost, given the benefits the taxpayers are getting.

Unless we have a revolution at the ballot box and people actually demand accountability and start questioning how their money is being spent, we'll have a continuation of the same policies and the same programs and the same politicians that got us into this mess in the first place.

PART FIVE

WHERE DO WE GO FROM HERE?

CHAPTER 25

CLASS ACTION

*B*y the time we were finished our journey we had concluded that all roads (despite diversions, detours and roadblocks) led to Ottawa and to the House on the Hill. It had become blatantly clear to us that, despite lessons learned, we had only taken our first step toward enlightenment. But we sensed that the ground already covered was nothing compared to the places we still had to go. But where to start?

It was obvious to us, given our newly acquired expertise, that the Canadians who made up the government were the only people who, one, could give us the answers we needed, and two, would, as soon as we pointed out the error of their ways, introduce more accountability into the system and solve all of our problems!

But how do you confront a government? It was one thing to get access to an empty House of Commons on a Saturday night. It was quite another thing to walk in during working hours, when we would undoubtedly be thrown out on our ears.

Back in Toronto while trying to decide our next move, someone recalled the comments that Ralph Hindson had made to us regarding the vested interests of politicians:

> In a company, if a subject comes up and you have a conflict of interest, you step out while it's being decided. But that doesn't happen in government. The politicians directly involved get even more involved .... I don't think politicians should be allowed to get involved in giving grants and large subsidies to companies .... Why Canadians don't do anything about this, I'm not sure. I have suggested a class action suit where people could take action against the government for doing things that they feel are not correct.

We took Mr. Hindson's suggestion and decided to face off against the government in a mock trial. Our idea was that the lawyers, including those for the defence, would be members of our own generation. The judge would be real and, if possible, we would film the proceedings in a real courtroom.

Patrick Boyer, a lawyer, professor and former member of parliament, became our M.R.C. (Mentor with the Right Connections). He introduced us to our lawyers, talked Judge Samuel Grange into adjudicating the session and convinced the chief justice of Ontario, Roy McMurtry, to allow us to film inside the law courts at Osgoode Hall in Toronto. The following is an edited transcript of the case.

— The Team

Kemp, Innes et al. versus the Government

Fade in.

INTERIOR: Courtroom number 10 at Osgoode Hall in downtown Toronto on a Saturday morning in June.

Sun streams through the windows, somehow at odds with the nature of the proceedings which are about to begin. Scaffolding, lights, cables and television cameras clutter the room, obscuring most of its ornate architecture. The lawyers for the plaintiffs are seated on the right facing the bench; those for the defendant, the government, are to the left. In the centre of this area there is a lectern with a microphone for the presentations by counsel. In front of the lectern and below the bench is the desk of the clerk of the court. There is a television set on the bench for the judge and two more sets have been placed on either side of the room for viewing the evidence of the witnesses. Spectators are seated behind the lawyers' desks. Paul Kemp and Jay Innes, who have brought this suit against the government on behalf of their generation, are sitting in the front row, immediately behind their lawyers. The government, however, is not represented except by counsel.

Clerk of the Court
All rise.

Judge Samuel Grange enters from his chambers and takes his place on the bench.

Clerk of the Court
Oyez, Oyez, Oyez. Anyone having business before the Queen's justice of this court, attend now and you shall be heard. Long live the Queen. Please be seated.

Kemp, Innes et al. versus the Government

Judge Samuel Grange addressing the jury (via the camera)
This trial in form perhaps is not like other trials, but it presents a real issue. The issue is a simple one. Did the governments of Canada, that is, the federal government and the provincial governments, so conduct the affairs of the nation as to do harm to a generation of Canadians, namely the present, younger generation, in particular by creating a large deficit the younger generation will have to repay? The form of this trial is somewhat different from normal. Normally evidence will be presented and will be subject to cross-examination. In this case the gathering of evidence has been by videotape and there will be no cross-examination.

Now, each side is represented by counsel. For the younger generation, the plaintiffs, Miss Tamar Pichette and Mr. Michael Neylan. And for the government, the defendant, Miss Kristan Taylor and Mr. John Fabello. All of these counsel will address you on one or other of the issues. It is important, however, to remember that they are advocates, not witnesses. What they say may well persuade you to believe certain facts and conclusions, but what they say is not by itself evidence. Miss Pichette, I believe you are to begin with the constitutional argument.

Tamar Pichette rises and takes her place at the lectern.

Tamar Pichette, Counsel for the Plaintiffs

Your Honour, our case begins with the assertion that the conduct of the Government of Canada, by creating a massive national debt by engaging in excessive overspending, has acted in violation of the Constitution of Canada. The Constitution empowers the government to raise funds by borrowing on the public credit and creates Parliament as an independent arm of government to control public spending. When government exercises its powers in a manner that is capricious and arbitrary, that conduct is subject to judicial scrutiny and to remedy by this court.

The evidence by the Dominion Bond Rating Service indicates that the federal debt level is clearly in excess of $570 billion. This amount does not include provincial debt, Crown corporation debt, municipal debt and unfunded liabilities. If you add in these numbers, the figure more than doubles. Our evidence clearly demonstrates that the government has deliberately and consistently exercised its power to borrow on the public credit in a manner that is both arbitrary and capricious. I refer the court to the evidence of Ken Dye, auditor general of Canada for 10 years.

> ### Witness: Ken Dye, Auditor General of Canada, 1981–1991
> Look at the pain we're enduring today with respect to the annual deficit, which was probably avoidable had somebody done something about it a decade ago when it was apparent. And people were concerned then, but action wasn't taken. Now, is that a great scandal? Or is it just bad management? Or is it good politics? I don't have the answer to that but we could have avoided all of this and had some other issue be the news of the day.

Question: So you were warning Parliament about some of the perils of this debt and deficit?

> Yes, and there's all kinds of evidence. I even drew pictures for them, graphs that showed the revenues like this and the expenditures like that. The debt curve going up ... these things were laid out so plainly that you couldn't fail to miss them.

Miss Pichette

Your Honour, clearly no effort was made to restrain spending. We are asking this court to make a clear declaration that the government, in permitting the national debt to grow unchecked, has violated the Constitution, has acted in excess of its constitutional powers and has failed to safeguard the interest of the citizens of Canada, in particular those younger generations whose money it has already spent in willful disregard of their interests. I refer you to the words of Charles Adams, tax historian and author.

Witness: Charles Adams, Tax Historian

You can't spend money you don't have and yet we find out that no, that's not true. Government can spend money it doesn't have. We can push this off on our great-grandchildren so they can pick up the tab. All we have to do is pay the interest. And of course that's outrageously immoral.

Miss Pichette

Your Honour, I equate the government's overspending to the behaviour of an addict eating bittersweet chocolate. The sweet is consumed and gone immediately and this generation is left with the bitter aftertaste of paying up. Your Honour, time is money and our time (and our money) is running out. Thank you.

Judge Grange

Thank you, Miss Pichette. Mr. Fabello, are you responding on this issue?

John Fabello, Counsel for the Defendant

Yes, thank you, Your Honour. By way of brief introduction, the government acknowledges that the plaintiffs have presented and will present some compelling evidence of the problems that face Canada today. However, the heart of this case is not whether the problems exist — they do — rather it is who is truly liable for their creation. The evidence will prove that the entire electorate of Canada has contributed to and caused the problems that are the impetus behind the plaintiffs' case.

I will now speak directly to the plaintiffs' submission with respect to the Constitution. The plaintiffs have argued that the government violated the Constitution because it spent excessively. The government submits that, quite simply, the government has done what it was told to do and therefore it should be viewed as fulfilling its constitutional duties, not breaching them. The government's conduct does not begin to approach capricious or arbitrary behaviour. The plaintiffs' characterization in this regard may have some dramatic appeal, but it's without substance. The true issue is, what caused the overspending? What caused my clients to take little action? To answer these questions you have to look at the very foundation of the Constitution, the principle of responsible government. Now, what is responsible government? Decisions are made by the members of the House of Commons who enjoy the confidence of the majority of that House, who are elected on the basis of universal adult suffrage. As such, the decision makers of the government are responsible to Canadian opinion, if they are doing their job. The government, if responsible, does what is demanded by the electorate.

The plaintiffs' own witness, Mr. Dye, has indicated that the government's activities that created the debt could simply be good politics, and he's right. The government has merely acted in accordance with the wishes, demands and requests of the people who voted it into power. And what has the electorate demanded? The very spending and the very programs that have caused the debt. Now, in making these demands the plaintiffs and the electorate have enjoyed the fruits of the spending and done nothing to remedy the problems caused thereby. The plaintiffs and the electorate have engaged in the same conduct of which they now complain.

Your Honour, you'll recall that the plaintiffs relied on the evidence of Mr. Adams for proof that overspending not only breaches the Constitution, but is immoral. However, the plaintiffs have failed to show you why Mr. Adams thinks it's immoral.

Witness: Charles Adams
It's immoral because we should pay for our own goods and services.

Mr. Fabello
That's right. We should pay, but the fact is, we have refused. I refer you now to the evidence of Brian Crowley, the president of the Atlantic Institute of Market Studies.

Witness: Brian Crowley, President of the Atlantic Institute of Market Studies
It's very easy to get benefits out of government. It's very easy for groups to organize and ask for a specific benefit, whether it's a tariff or a wage subsidy or a subsidy to investment. Whatever it is,

it's very hard for government to stop paying a benefit once they've started because paying a benefit creates a group that has an interest in keeping that benefit and they will lobby till the cows come home in order to defend that interest. Now, what's happened is the size of government has grown, and more and more of us are all receiving some kind of good or service from government that is subsidized by the general taxpayer, and believe me, every one of us in some way is involved in a taking activity.

Mr. Fabello
Yes, we demand the costly benefits. We take them, we use them and we refuse to let them go. Indeed, and I'm quoting Mr. Crowley, "We will lobby till the cows come home to keep them." I refer you to the evidence of Alan Ross, the former senior assistant deputy minister of supply and services, and Donald Savoie, author and professor of public administration at the University of Moncton.

> **Witness: Alan Ross, Former Senior Assistant Deputy Minister of Supply and Services**
> We had a generation of Canadians who drove politicians, who had great expectations, who insisted that government become more involved in the issues of Canadians, whether it be grants to business, whether it be subsidies, whether it be immigration. It doesn't matter what it was, there was an acceptance by the public generally that the government's going to look after us.

> **Witness: Donald Savoie, Author of *Governing from the Centre***
> I think the private sector in many instances has been a complete fraud. Businesspeople will fly down and argue, "Cut spending," but they'll be first at the trough.

Mr. Fabello
Indeed! Here is another image, my Lord, that I would like you to keep in mind. We are all at the trough and refuse, in our gluttony, to look up.

Your Honour, those are my submissions with respect to the constitutional argument.

Judge Grange
Thank you, Mr. Fabello. Mr. Neylan, I believe you are speaking on the subject of negligence.

Michael Neylan, Counsel for the Plaintiffs

Thank you, Your Honour. We contend that for the past 25 years the government has been negligent. The government has been negligent by engaging in excessive spending that has crippled an entire generation by the creation of a massive debt.

One of the most obvious examples of negligence is the failure of the government to account for the manner in which it spends money or incurs expenses on behalf of the public. The government's method of accounting is acknowledged by former government officials to be incomprehensible, utterly incomprehensible. Consider, for example, the evidence of Paul Dick, a member of Parliament for 23 years, who characterized this system of accounting as a third language that nobody understands.

> **Witness: Paul Dick, Minister of Supply and Services, 1989–1993**
> The Estimates of today are in a form that 99.9 percent of the people of this country haven't a clue how to read. It's a third language. Its not French, it's not English. It's accounting, but nobody understands it. You would at least understand the statements of Bell Canada or Alcan or one of the banks, but nobody except bureaucrats understands the public accounts and the Estimates procedures.

Question: Are you saying that even accountants don't understand this language?

> That's true. As a matter of fact, at one stage I got the managing partners of each of the six major accounting firms in the Ottawa area to come and sit on the committee with me, and five out of the six said they did not understand the government's accounting or the government books. They could not read them.

Mr. Neylan

As you can see, the basic foundation of fiscal responsibility is absent from the practices of government. We seriously have to ask ourselves, "Is this baffling system of public accounting deliberate?"

Let's consider how the government has been spending our money. It's been funnelling tax dollars to regions of Canada that suffer from historic levels of unemployment by investing in projects that ultimately go broke. It has been providing direct and indirect support for businesses with subsidies causing these businesses to become falsely dependent on government and to lose their competitive advantage. The government has been granting monopoly powers to Crown corporations, which, without competition, do not need to account to the taxpayers. What we have discovered is that government is in the business of subsidizing dependency and that this has created a nation that is immunized from change. I refer, Your Honour, to the evidence of Michael MacDonald, the former vice president of the federal government's regional development agency, ACOA (the Atlantic Canada Opportunities Agency).

Witness: Michael MacDonald, Former President of ACOA

If you look at the history of all these agencies and all these initiatives and all these federal programs, it's not cynical to conclude that the Government of Canada is not in the economic development business, it's in the dependency business. I think that if you rely on somebody else for their ideas, if you rely on them for direction, if you rely on them for dollars and if you rely on them for continued support, you pay a phenomenal personal, cultural and moral price.

Mr. Neylan

The problem is, once subsidies exist they're particularly hard to get rid of, and I refer you to the evidence of Brian Crowley, who stated that handouts encourage people to drop out of a productive economy.

Witness: Brian Crowley

It seems to me that we have created a system in which it is easy for people to drop out of the productive economy. If we take people on unemployment insurance as an example, the trend has been upward even during boom years. After the recession at the beginning of the 1980s, we enjoyed six or seven years of really stellar economic growth. But the number of unemployment insurance beneficiaries continued to go up.

Mr. Neylan

One last example of negligence, probably the most distressing of all, is the willful blindness on the part of both federal and provincial governments in ignoring for the past 25 years the compounding effects of interest. As a result, we're left with the staggering realization that this year the federal government's greatest expenditure will be to pay interest on the debt. This is referred to by Walter Schroeder, president of the Dominion Bond Rating Service.

Witness: Walter Schroeder, President of the Dominion Bond Rating Service
Ninety percent [of the debt] is due to compounding interest and seven percent is due to program expenditure being higher than program revenue. The other three percent is the debt that was outstanding as of March 31, 1965. So we're in a very, very unhappy position today.

Mr. Neylan

Thirty-five cents of every tax dollar goes, not to help the poor, not to pay for health care, not to improve the lot of the average citizen, but instead to cover interest payments on the national debt. Imagine what those payments could do for this country if that debt did not exist. Imagine this, and understand why we are in the courtroom today. Thank you, Your Honour.

Judge Grange

Thank you, Mr. Neylan. Mr. Fabello, are you responding?

Mr. Fabello

I am, Your Honour. The government submits, Your Honour, assuming for the moment that its conduct amounts to negligence, that the electorate, through its conduct, has voluntarily accepted the risks associated with the government's actions and has contributed to, if not caused, the damage complained of. In short, the actions of the electorate and the plaintiffs have amounted to negligence because they have blindly and selfishly demanded benefits, subsidies and government programs.

Your Honour, if you will recall the evidence of Messrs. Savoie and Crowley — Mr. Crowley stated that people "will lobby till the cows come home" to keep their benefits and subsidies, and Mr. Savoie said that the private sector, while giving lip service to the idea of reducing spending, will often "be the first at the trough" lining up for more government largesse. To blend the metaphors they've used, Mr. Crowley and Mr. Savoie paint a picture of cows at the trough, recklessly slopping up all the feed they can get without regard for the inevitable consequences of doing so. Not a pretty picture, but entirely accurate. Your Honour, as John Crosbie and Michael MacDonald indicate, the plaintiffs' generation, along with the rest of the population, has contributed to the negligence that has caused the problems.

Witness: John Crosbie,
Former Conservative MP and Cabinet Minister
The public is the author of its own misfortunes. They are getting what they bloody well deserve because they don't expect any better.

Witness: Michael MacDonald
In areas of responsibility we are responsible for ourselves. We shouldn't blame Ottawa. We did it, we wanted it, and we collaborated in the weakening of our country. We're collaborators.

Mr. Fabello

Indeed, we are collaborators. We are responsible. We must accept responsibility. The plaintiffs have argued that the government has ignored checks and balances on its conduct. Well, the plaintiffs' analysis ignores the fact that the electorate has at its disposal a most effective check — the vote. The government submits, Your Honour, that all the plaintiffs need to do is look in the mirror and they will see who holds the key to effecting change. As Jason Kenney indicates, the electorate should stop playing the victim and change its conduct, which for the most part has been marked with inertia and lethargy.

Witness: Jason Kenney, Former Director of the Canadian Taxpayers Association
People have to expect less and demand less from government. But they also have to get involved in the system so that politicians hear from more than just the squeaky wheels who want more spending and begin to hear consistently from those who want government to live within its means.

Mr. Fabello

Your Honour, those are my submissions with respect to negligence.

Judge Grange

Thank you. Miss Pichette, you are speaking on breach of trust?

Miss Pichette

Yes, Your Honour, thank you.

The defendant seeks to shift blame for the debt onto the Canadian people, the electorate. The fact is that once the government is in office, it has a duty. We are alleging breach of trust by the government.

To put it at its simplest, the government is the guardian of public funds. It acts as trustee of those funds, which are paid by Canadians in the expectation of future benefits. It is our position that in its role as trustee, the government must be held accountable for the mismanagement, the dissipation, the waste of those funds. This court has heard evidence that the government believed it was acting in the best interests of the Canadian people. The implication is that it has therefore, honourably, and with integrity, discharged its duties in using public funds. Your Honour, that is a patent lie.

Consider the Canada Pension Plan. A private pension plan is required by law to have enough assets to cover current and future obligations. The Canada Pension Plan, in contrast, is subject to no such regulation. The Canada Pension Plan has never been fully funded because the politicians assumed they could arbitrarily use the power of taxation and borrowing to make up any later shortfall. The government knew as early as the mid-1970s that the plan was grossly underfunded. It deliberately chose not to do anything. I refer you to the evidence of David Slater, the former general director of the federal Finance Department.

> **Witness: David Slater, Former General Director of the Department of Finance**
> Back between 1978 and 1981 there was a massive series of studies of the retirement-income system in Canada, and they universally agreed that if we did nothing, we were going to be in a situation where the payments in were going to have to increase just to maintain the benefits. Everybody knew then that someday, sooner or later, there would have to be an increase in the contribution rates. What clearly happened, of course, is that we did nothing. The whole issue was postponed. If the matter had been tackled earlier, it would have been a less serious problem now.

Miss Pichette
Your Honour, in the case of the Canada Pension Plan, at least we can say that some government officials bothered to inform themselves about how bad the situation was before they chose not to do anything. For other social welfare programs offered by the federal government, nobody even bothered to obtain estimates for the long-term costs of the programs. I refer you to the evidence of Paul McCrossan, who became a member of Parliament in 1978.

Witness: Paul McCrossan, Actuary and Former MP
The Old Age Security program has never been estimated for more than a year and a half in advance as far as I can find out. The Guaranteed Income Supplement was never estimated until the late 1980s, and the cost of medicare, to my knowledge, has never been estimated to this day.

We brought in a lot of social programs figuring they were self-sustaining, but nobody actually prepared the figures to determine if they could be afforded in the long run, until 1986.

Miss Pichette
The reason for this conduct is simple: votes. The more the politicians appear to be creating immediate benefits for the public [without regard for the future], the greater their popularity and their chances of re-election. We have heard evidence of the politicians' agenda, the visibility attendant upon going to their home constituency to say, "Look what I've got for you!"

Witness: Tom McMillan, Former Conservative Cabinet Minister
What we were doing was mortgaging the future of our children and their children and children yet unborn. But as politicians all we were concerned about was the next election. Vision for a politician is the next election. Eternity is the election after that, and beyond such a scope I don't think politicians have the capacity to give much thought to decisions that are being made.

Miss Pichette
Your Honour, politicians are using our tax dollars to buy votes. I refer the court to the evidence of Catherine Swift, president of the Canadian Federation of Independent Business, who reveals the political motivation behind the granting of subsidies.

Witness: Catherine Swift, President of the Canadian Federation of Independent Business
Subsidies tend to be motivated more by a politician wanting to hand over a cheque and shake somebody's hand in front of some media cameras, and they tend to be motivated by pork barrelling so that the person gets re-elected next time around. They are rarely, if ever, motivated by good, sound economic reasons. Goodness knows, in Canadian history we can count numerous instances where we have literally thrown billions and

billions and billions of dollars into sinkholes. The resource sector is full of examples of companies that didn't survive because they weren't viable.

Miss Pichette
Clearly the politicians' interest in getting re-elected conflicts with the public interest. The law says that where trustees' interests conflict with those of their beneficiaries, they must either excuse themselves or be held to the highest standard of care and loyalty with respect to the beneficiaries' interests. Therefore, Your Honour, it would not be inconceivable, in light of the pervasive and ongoing nature of its conduct, to ask that the government excuse itself, step down, on the grounds that it has acted in conflict with the interests of the generation we represent. It has failed to uphold the highest standard of care and loyalty in managing public funds; it has failed to ensure that the younger generation of beneficiaries will receive anything at all in return for the contributions they make. We are asking this court to make a mandatory order requiring the government to rectify the situation.

Earlier I stated that the government's conduct was like that of an addict who had gorged himself on chocolate. This generation cannot bear any greater weight, not in its tax contributions nor in its pension contributions. It's time to put the government on a diet. Thank you, Your Honour.

Judge Grange
Thank you, Miss Pichette. Miss Taylor, would you like to respond?

Kristan Taylor, Counsel for the Defendant
Yes, Your Honour, thank you. The plaintiffs have made grave allegations attacking the government's integrity. Their allegations lack substance and they lack merit. The government recognizes its role as a trustee of public funds. The question before you is whether the government has breached this trust. My client maintains, and the evidence shows, that it has acted as it must in accordance with the trust. The argument presented by the plaintiffs is deceptively simple: something is rotten in the state of Canada and the government must be to blame. But is it? Basic trust principles require trustees to honestly exercise their best judgment according to the mandate of the trust. The first principle does not hold a trustee to a standard of perfection or infallibility. Consider the evidence of William Teron, former president of the Canada Mortgage and Housing Corporation.

Witness: William Teron, Former President of the Canada Mortgage and Housing Corporation
If a good idea came forward, the government virtually jumped at the great opportunity to do good, and at that time they honestly felt that they were doing good. And they were, in the short run. But I don't think any of them actually projected themselves and saw there was an end to the rainbow.

Miss Taylor
Mr. Teron's evidence attests to the honesty of the government in financing public programs. We are not here to argue that the government's actions have been perfect; no, we freely admit that what happened, happened. The plaintiffs, though, have developed a theory that there has been a conspiracy against the younger generation. Consider the words of someone who speaks with authority, having been a member of Parliament himself: Tom McMillan.

Witness: Tom McMillan
There's no conspiracy here. It's not some kind of plot brewed in a cauldron by politicians in Ottawa. The public is as much to blame as the politicians and the bureaucrats because they condone it; they even demand it.

Miss Taylor
"They even demand it." The government's mandate is defined by the Canadian people's demands. In any democracy founded on responsible government, a covenant exists between the government and the governed. The government must be responsible to its citizens and the citizens must define the government's mandate and hold it accountable.

With respect to the Canada Pension Plan, Canadians gave the government the mandate to create a universal pension program. The government implemented the program and it worked. Now, admittedly, the program has run into some serious problems, but did the government conceal this knowledge from the beneficiaries of the program? Not at all. The plaintiffs' evidence shows that the public knew this was coming all along. David Slater, whom they rely upon, openly acknowledged that studies revealed flaws in the Canada Pension Plan over 15 years ago. The information was available but no change was made. Consider, in this regard, the testimony of Paul Dick, former minister of supply and services.

217

Witness: Paul Dick
Nobody has insisted on a better program. The politicians haven't, the people of Canada haven't, the press hasn't.

Miss Taylor
Nobody insisted on a better program. The national mind was effectively in neutral, Your Honour. The citizens of Canada had a responsibility to change the government's mandate and Canadians did not do so. The plaintiffs have accused the politicians of having ulterior, suspect motives — they were pork barrelling, they were buying votes.

But what would have happened if the government had put change on the agenda without the agreement of the public? It would have suffered the same fate as that suffered by other governments that attempted to implement unpopular measures — defeat! I refer you to the evidence of the Honourable John Crosbie, former minister of finance, who suffered such a fate in 1979.

Witness: John Crosbie
If you say to the public, "Look, vote for me; I'm going to get in. We've got a serious financial problem and I'm going to have to do x, y, and z to cut back and we're going to have to stop this too-lavish unemployment insurance and make changes in the social security system," they will vote against you. The public simply will not support you if you sell them on that basis.

Miss Taylor
The authenticity of John Crosbie's evidence is fully supported by another former member of Parliament, Paul McCrossan.

Witness: Paul McCrossan
When Mr. Crosbie said that the budget deficit was a serious issue, he proposed a tax of 4¢ a litre to raise the price of gasoline from 18¢ a litre to 22¢ a litre, which seems laughable by today's standards. There was a massive rejection by the taxpayers. They just didn't want to have anything to do with taxes to control the deficit and they didn't want to have anything to do with cutting back the benefits either. And of course the government was defeated.

Miss Taylor
The people didn't want to control the deficit. The government, therefore, has not breached its trust with the younger generation, Your Honour, the people of Canada have. The plaintiffs have sued the wrong party.

Judge Grange
Thank you, Miss Taylor. Mr. Neylan, will you proceed to the subject of unjust enrichment.

Mr. Neylan
Yes, Your Honour. Regardless of all that is said and done, one generation has been unjustly enriched at the expense of another, and it would be an injustice to leave that burden to the younger generation. The older generation has enjoyed the party while we suffer the hangover. Your Honour, the government has engaged in vast public borrowing against the future credit of this country and brought new meaning to the phrase "robbing the cradle."

The Canada Pension Plan is an excellent example of unjust enrichment. Because the plan operated as a pay-as-you-go system, the massive liabilities that have accrued do not show up on the government books. They are merely a promise to pay sometime in the future, and like other promises to pay made in the 1970s and 80s, that cost will be borne by the younger generation.

Deficit financing is an even greater injustice. The government has incurred an incredible debt, $570 million, spending it for the benefit of one generation while leaving us to pick up the tab. Deficit financing has meant that over the past 25 years Canadians have not fully paid for their services or for the subsidies they have received. Now, the honest thing would have been to raise taxes or cut spending. Instead, the government chose to pass those costs on to future generations. They handed the bill to their children and those children are now facing the largest expenditure on the books — the payment of interest on the debt. It is submitted that to borrow for the benefit of one generation for its sole benefit at the expense of another is utterly irresponsible and dangerous. Here again is David Slater, the former general director of the Department of Finance, speaking of the Canada Pension Plan.

Witness: David Slater
The danger is a real intergenerational conflict because young people today see that they have ahead of them the prospect of

paying huge increases in contributions without getting comparable improvements in their benefits. They are going to be footing the bill for the older people, and indeed they are getting a very bad deal in terms of the pay-in they make and the benefits that they are going to receive.

Mr. Neylan
Now consider the words of Jason Kenney.

> **Witness: Jason Kenney**
> I think that over the next 10 or 15 years you'll see the younger generation, those moving into the workforce, becoming increasingly aware of the growing burden. And you're going to see younger people finally wake up to the fact that they've been robbed, that there's been intergenerational theft going on here for two or three decades.

Mr. Neylan
Theft! That's exactly what it is. The older generation has saddled us with debt. Is it fair to tell us now that we must work that much harder just to ensure that they have a comfortable retirement? Your Honour, this court can put an end to this theft by granting the relief sought to the younger generation, and it can stop the intergenerational conflict that has put us in this courtroom today. Thank you.

Judge Grange
Miss Taylor, will you give a proper response?

Miss Taylor
I certainly will, Your Honour. Intergenerational theft! These are inflammatory words, Your Honour, but they are words that lack foundation.

Contrary to what you've heard from my learned friend, the government is not in the business of "robbing the cradle." What the government has done, and what the public has compelled the government to do, is to protect Canadians from the cradle to the grave! The plaintiffs' generation is no exception. As earlier indicated by Brian Crowley, we are all involved in a taking activity. Can the plaintiffs seriously believe that they are somehow immune from this? They too have benefited. Education is the most obvious example of this. Consider the evidence of Professor Filip Palda.

Witness: Filip Palda, Professor of Public Administration
I have been feeding off government quite heavily most of my
life. I got a wonderful education in the States that was largely
paid for by the Canadian government. I take the train between
Montreal and Toronto maybe once a week and that train is subsidized by the Canadian government. I'm not complaining, and
I'm not the only one who benefits from these middle-class entitlements. You are benefiting from them, or have benefited, if
you pass through the university system. Students who go to
university think they are paying for their education, but they're
only paying about a tenth of the cost of their education. The
rest is being picked up by the taxpayers.

Miss Taylor
Can the younger generation really have the audacity to accuse the government of deprivation, having indulged in all the benefits of such a
generous educational system? It's far easier to blame the government
than to accept a share of the broader responsibility. Consider the evidence of Charles Adams.

Witness: Charles Adams
People have got to have it drummed into their heads. If you're
going to rebel over taxes, then you're going to have to accept
that you're not going to get the entitlements and you're not
going to get the public expenditure that is causing the taxes in
the first place, and worse than that, causing the deficit that is
bankrupting the country. So somebody has got to hammer on
them to get their heads screwed on right because that's what the
problem is.

Miss Taylor
An acceptance of responsibility is required. There is a valid explanation
for what has happened in this country. We demanded it, and I use the
word in the broadest possible sense. I am a member of the plaintiffs'
generation and I include myself in that "we." We, as Canadian citizens,
demanded excessive spending, demanded the proliferation of ultimately
unsustainable social programs.

Our insatiable demands caused these problems. Our inaction perpetu-
ated them. We all must share in the blame. The plaintiffs have not suffered deprivation and there is a valid explanation for the state of this

country today. They have not, therefore, established a case for unjust enrichment. Those are my submissions.

Judge Grange
Thank you, Miss Taylor. Now, Mr. Neylan, will you sum up for the plaintiffs?

Mr. Neylan
Thank you, Your Honour. The violation of constitutional principles, negligence, breach of trust, unjust enrichment — these grounds, based on the evidence presented to this court, clearly require that the younger generation obtain relief. Their situation is best summed up in a speech given by the lieutenant governor of Ontario in 1993, wherein he said:

> It is ... difficult for me, speaking to you today as a representative of our nation's leadership, in all conscience to confess to you that my generation owes to you, the younger generation of today, an abject apology. We owe you for having to a very real extent, mortgaged your future to satisfy our present wants. We owe you for fuelling your expectations to grow far beyond our power to fulfill them. Your generation will therefore have to work harder and be even more productive simply to pay the interest on our overindulgence.

Your Honour, an apology will not suffice. For members of my generation to be told that they must work harder and be more productive simply to pay off the interest on the older generation's overindulgence is both morally and legally repugnant!

Judge Grange
Thank you, Mr. Neylan. Miss Taylor, I will now hear your summation for the defendant.

Miss Taylor
Your Honour, today the plaintiffs have exposed a problem of great magnitude. The government admits that problem. As I've said before, what happened, happened. We are not here today to make excuses for it. What my clients dispute, however, is the plaintiffs' interpretation of the evidence and where they seek to lay the blame. The evidence does not point the finger at the government. It points far beyond the government. The real culprits, from whom the plaintiffs should be seeking redress, are the Canadian people. The citizens of this country must be held accountable

for the mess it is in today. The government action has been prompted and fuelled by public demand. Canadians are the accomplices, they are the collaborators and, indeed, at times have been the instigators.

In their journey across the country, speaking with Canadians to find out what went wrong, the plaintiffs discovered that all Canadians, whether they know it or not, are deeply dependent on the government. This dependency has grown to the point that today it goes unrecognized. But what the plaintiffs have failed to realize is that their generation is included and that the government is not the place to lay the blame. Remember the evidence of John Crosbie. He said, "The public is the author of its own misfortunes. People are getting what they bloody well deserve because they don't expect any better."

He's right. We get exactly what we bloody well deserve.

Your Honour, the issue before this court is accountability. Who is responsible? The government? Certainly! But this case goes beyond the government and it goes beyond the parameters of this courtroom. The plaintiffs have put the government on trial, but I believe what they've really done is put the country on trial.

This trial does not belong in a court of law. It is a trial for the court of public opinion, and the government invites, no, the government encourages the plaintiffs to take it there!

Judge Grange
Thank you, Miss Taylor. We'll recess now for a few minutes while I consider the matter.

Clerk of the Court
All rise. Court stands recessed for 15 minutes.

Fifteen minutes later.

Clerk of the Court
Order. All rise. Court is resumed. Please be seated.

Judge Grange addressing the jury
Now you have heard the case for the plaintiffs, the younger generation, and the defendant, the government.

The case for the plaintiffs, simply put, is that the government has irresponsibly, indeed, illegally, negligently, unconstitutionally and in breach of trust enriched itself and the citizens and constituents of this country from time to time, so that now there is a huge debt which must be paid by the generation that the plaintiffs represent.

The case for the defendant is not that they didn't do what is alleged but that what they did was at the behest of their constituents, the older generation who empowered them and were the beneficiaries of the government's largesse. The older generation are the true defendants who must bear the responsibility.

To deal with the particulars, the plaintiffs state that the government has been arbitrary in its borrowing on the public credit and has wildly over-borrowed contrary to the Constitution. The defence says that the borrowing has been to satisfy the insatiable demands of the public and there is no constitutional violation in doing just that.

The plaintiffs allege that the government has been negligent, particularly in the handling of subsidies and having controls on spending. The government says the plaintiffs have contributed to or even caused the negligence by lobbying, demanding benefits and failing to effect a possible change.

The plaintiffs say the government has acted in breach of trust by mismanaging and wasting public funds, and note particularly the failure to fund properly the Canada Pension Plan, passing the burden on to future generations. Defence says there has been no breach of trust: the government has acted in accordance with its best judgment and in accord with its mandate, which the public declined to change.

The plaintiffs argue that the older generation has become unjustly enriched at the expense of the younger generation. The defence then points out that the younger generation has taken advantage of all the programs offered and must share the responsibility for the debt.

As I said at the outset, this trial is somewhat exceptional. We have conducted it as close to a regular trial as the circumstances will permit and now we must consider your participation, you, the jury, to whom we now turn over the case. You must determine on the evidence, assisted by the argument of counsel, whether the case for the plaintiffs or that of the defendant will prevail. I ask you to consider all of the evidence, weigh all of the arguments and then, to the best of your ability and in accordance with your consciences, reach the best, the most just, verdict that you can. Thank you all very much.

Clerk of the Court
Order. All rise. Oyez, Oyez. Oyez. The sittings of this court are now concluded. God save the Queen.

Judge Grange retires to his chambers. The lawyers shake hands with Jay and Paul and the courtroom slowly empties.

Fade to black.

After the trial — without a verdict, but with new insights, refocused energy and a broader view of the problems confronting all Canadians — we hit the road again. Years have passed; elections have been held; the party rules; the journey continues.

As far as we know, the jury is still out.

— The Team

INDEX